Janet Winter has been involved in costuming activities since she was five years old, when she discovered sheets and safety pins. Since then, she has expanded her interests in historical costuming to include designing and making costumes for several plays put on by local theater groups. She has also acted in and made historical clothing for the California Renaissance and Dickens Faires since 1967, as well as for Dance Thru Time, a historical dance troupe. In her copious free time, she works full time, is Art Director of *The Grenadier* magazine, and raises two children plus various pets at her home in Oakland. Her hobby is what you are holding in your hands.

Carolyn Schultz Savoy is a graduate of the California College of Arts and Crafts. Her degree is in Environmental Design, so naturally, she is a costumer. She has always been involved with costume design, in one way or another, whether draping costumes on dolls ("I didn't play with dolls, except for that."), Halloween costumes, or theatrical costumes. She became interested in historical re-creations after meeting Janet Winter in 1978. From 1980 through 1982, Carolyn was the Director of Costuming for the Living History Centre, producers of the Renaissance Pleasure Faires. She now does freelance costume and illustration as well as continuing her search for the perfect fine-point sketch pen.

ELIZABETHAN COSTUMING

FOR THE YEARS 1550-1580

TO OUR READERS

We hope you will read the first section of this book, before going on to the how-to sections, because people are more than just clothes. They live and work and play in their world, and we are attempting to put the Elizabethans into the world they lived in, as well as the clothes they wore, so that you can understand them better as people.

JANET WINTER & CAROLYN SAVOY

Illustrated by Carolyn Schultz Savoy

Second Edition

Other Times Publications
Oakland, California

Also from Other Times Productions:

Victorian Costuming: Volume I
1840-1865

Coming soon:

Medieval Costuming: Volume I
1066-1300

Elizabethan Costuming
ISBN 0-9630220-0-8

This book is dedicated to Doris Karnes of the Living History Centre, and our friends, especially Rod & Arthur & Michael, who nagged us until we sat down to write this book, then nagged us some more, until we finished it.

INTRODUCTION

This book will show you how to design and construct the basic garments for the different social classes in Elizabethan England. It will not tell you how to make a costume, because this is not a costume that you will be making and wearing. You will be dressing yourself in the clothing of another time, and it will feel more natural to you if you think of it in that way. After all, *they* wore it every day, all their lives, and felt perfectly normal in it. They weren't wearing costumes, and neither will you when you are dressed in it. It will just be clothing. The more you wear it, around the house or working in the garden, the more lived in it will feel and look.

Before this book gets into the specifics of garments and their construction, it will tell you something of the immediate history of England in the 16th Century and the lifestyle of the Elizabethans so you will understand the why of things that were done. If you understand why the Elizabethans did things a certain way in their clothing, you will be able to design and work out more authentic garments for yourself that will be more expressive of yourself and any character you want to portray.

FORWARD TO THE SECOND EDITION

To err is human, and in the first edition of this book we discovered our humanity all too well in some of the comments made by our readers. We have taken your feedback into consideration in the production of this second edition.

We have also set the book up a little differently so that it should be easier to use. The larger format means that the book should lie flat at the page you are trying to consult, and we have separated the men's and women's clothing sections for greater clarity.

We have added notes on military influences, children's dress, and tricks of the trade. There is a generalized pattern section, so that you can find specific patterns based on pictures of garment types, rather than having to try to find an outdated pattern at your fabric store. We have included some sources of things for those of you who may have trouble finding things such as hoopwire, boning, hook tape and the like.

For the nit-pickers among you, we have left at least one misspelled word in the text, so you will have something to nit-pick about. For the rest of you, use the book and enjoy it.

First Edition, 1979
Revised Edition, 1983

TABLE OF CONTENTS

SECTION I: BACKGROUND

CAPSULE HISTORY

When the War of the Roses ended in 1485, England spent some 25 years licking its wounds and recovering from the longest civil war it had ever known. By the time that Henry VIII came to the throne in 1509, his father, Henry VII, had managed to consolidate the Tudor's position on the throne, stabilize the money system, and generally bring the country back on an even keel.

Henry VIII made England a nation to be reckoned with in the courts of Europe. A brilliant politician, he inherited a country made rich by his father's parsimonious habits and he spent money freely to impress the world with England's wealth and power. Then, after twenty years on the throne, he tore the country apart by founding the Anglican Church and dissolving the monastaries. He disbanded the Catholic Church in England and confiscated its wealth for the Crown.

His son, Edward, was only ten years old when he came to the throne and was ruled in all things by his councillors. He strengthened the position of the Anglican Church, but accomplished little of note before dying six years later.

Mary Tudor, on the other hand, did her best to demolish the infant Church and reintroduce Roman Catholicism. Her marriage to Philip II of Spain drained her country of its resources and came close to destroying it politically in the eyes of the world. England's money was debased and the country was nearly bankrupt when she died in 1558.

Elizabeth's ascension gave England a sense of relief from the religious and political upheavals of the previous 25 years. Her first task was the re-establish the Anglican Church and restore the people's belief in the coinage. She was a firm but moderate monarch who never allowed the extremists of any party to gain the upper hand. There was a new rising tide of nationalism which combined with a sense of destiny that expressed itself in a fever of exploration and claiming of new lands for the Crown.

With the dissolution of the monastaries in Henry's time, more money, formerly that of the Church's, came into secular hands, most often into the hands of the Crown and its court. From the Court, the money made its way into the hands of the growing middle class. More efficent farming techniques meant that less of the population had to work the land in order to feed all of the people. This made many of the more ambitious move to the cities in order to find new opportunities, which were abundant. The cities, primarily London, grew by leaps and bounds throughout the 16th Century and the middle class grew with it.

2

Elizabeth I

It was a time of conspicuous consumption in many things.
The rich were very rich and even the poor were relatively well
off compared with the Continent. Few people died of starvation,
though many were undernourished. England was also the home of
a thriving wool industry. Henry VIII had encouraged the growth
of the wool trade and his daughter did the same by requiring
every man to wear a wool cap on Sundays. Wool cloth was cheap
and plentiful, so few but the poorest went badly clothed.

Henry VIII had begun an enormous quantity of building during his reign, which employed thousands of artists and craftsmen, many of them English. Elizabeth did no major building of
her own, but her courtiers engaged in a riot of construction

during her reign which was typified by the emergence of the country house as an art form and lifestyle.

Clothing expressed a growing confidence of the people in their physical and spiritual abilities to control their own destinies. The Tudor Court declared in fashion its supremacy over things of the earth. Previous fashions had used gracefully flowing fabrics, close-clinging styles, and high-reaching headresses to indicate an upward striving toward Heaven. The bulkier, more down-to-earth styles, introduced by the court of Henry VIII, were modified by Elizabeth's courtiers into a less unnatural line, but were still expressive of their increased control over their environment. The middle class imitated their betters as much as their purses and the sumptuary laws would allow. The poor wore what was left over or discarded; or the extremely simplified versions of the richer styles, often as much as 50 years behind fashion's lastest dictates.

Edward IV Medieval

Henry VIII   Early Tudor

CLASS STRUCTURE & SUMPTUARY LAWS

All during the Middle Ages, the Renaissance, and even well into the 19th century, there was a very real and relatively rigid class structure throughout society. A person was born into a certain class and was expected to maintain this place through his entire life.

To the Elizabethan mind everything had its place. It was called "The Great Chain of Being". It gave people a great feeling of security because one always knew who was above and who was below oneself. The Great Chain started at the bottom with rocks and minerals, followed by plants, then the beasts of forest and field. Peasants were above the beasts, followed by the middle class, gentry, nobility and peers of the realm, in that order. The Queen was the highest earthly being in their eyes; she did God's will on Earth. After her, came all the many degrees of angels and archangels, and at the pinnacle, God.

5

Some upward mobility, as well as the reverse was possible, but most folks stayed in the same class as their parents and were content to remain so. The place he lived, the work he did, the type of woman he married, how he dressed, and even what he ate and drank during his lifetime was determined by the rules of conduct for his class. This was accepted by the majority of the population as God's Will, and many of the rules of society were set up to maintain this status quo.

Some of the rules were called Sumptuary Laws, equivalent to a luxury tax. These laws were essentially a mandatory dress code for the different classes within society. They said that a person could not dress above his station in the style of his garment, the type or color of fabric, trim or decoration of his clothing, in any way. For example; only the Queen could wear true purple; a person of the middle classes could wear no gold or silver trim or embroidery on his clothing; true black or bright jewel-like tones of dye were taxed; a peasant could wear no fur trim on his clothes at all; and no lady of the Court could out-dress the Queen at any time. One lady had her ears boxed in public by the Royal Fist once, because her gown was more ornate than the Queen's own.

People who wanted to get around the laws for whatever reason could pay a fine, called the sumptuary tax, and then they could wear, within reason, whatever they wanted and could afford. This is why you can see so many portraits of wealthy merchants who are dressed in a manner well above their actual station in life. They were willing to pay the tax in order to dress sumptuously.

The effect of these laws was that you could usually tell the station of a person at a glance and know immediately how you should react to him. It tended to make life much simpler, because proper behavior to a person above or below you was vastly more important than it is now. It could mean your very life, or at least a beating to slight a touchy noble. Fortunes sometimes hung on the correct degree of reverance to a superior. Knowing the class of a stranger you were greeting made it easier to deal with him correctly.

WEATHER & LIFESTYLE

England, in Northern Europe, is a cold country with average daytime temperatures in the summer of 55-65 degrees. It is cloudy and often rains or drizzles no matter what the season. The lack of intense summer sun means that English ladies have some of the finest and palest complexions in the world. The English always dress warmly and carry umbrellas for good reason.

In Elizabeth's time, England was 5-10 degrees colder than it is today, and central heating was unknown. Therefore people dressed in layers, ate prodigiously, and were very active. Everybody did a lot of walking, as it was necessary as well as recreational, even for the nobles. Most horses were owned by the upper classes and there were no public coaches at this time. If people wanted to get someplace, they walked. The nobles and others with leisure time tended to play active games and hunted on horseback nearly every day. Everybody danced, and most of the dances were very lively. The Queen took a brisk walk and danced a galliard before breakfast early every morning until shortly before she died at age 69.

Most theatrical, costumed events nowadays, whether indoors or outdoors, take place in a climate which is considerably warmer and/or sunnier than 16th century England. This means that people who wish to dress like Elizabethans may find themselves wilting from the heat. This is especially true during all-day outdoor events, such as the various Renaissance Faires or Shakespeare Festivals that take place during the summer season all around the country.

If you, the participant or attendee, want to look the part of a proper Elizabethan, but don't want to keel over by mid-day, you will have to make some practical compromise between authenticity and comfort. Use lighter weight fabrics or fewer layers to start with. Design your clothing so that parts may be removed in the heat of the day. The Elizabethans did this for their own comfort, and if it worked for them, it will work for you.

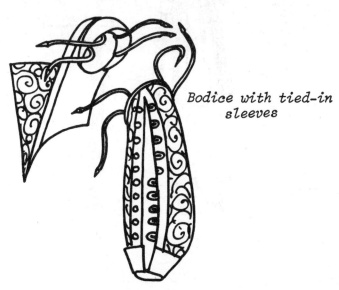

Bodice with tied-in sleeves

For example - due to the fashionable stiff corsetry and equally tight-fitting sleeves of this period, movement could be extremely limited, so many sleeves on gowns and doublets were tied or laced into the armholes with ribands, also called points, rather than sewn in. Also, even the most well-to-do had only a few basic garments with many sleeves and other accessories to change the look for different seasons or social occasions. The basic garments were made to last for years and because styles changed slowly, a person could wear the same garment for a decade and still be in fashion with new sleeves, hat, and accessories.

Good ideas never die. Take a look at a rack of new ski parkas and you will find that many have sleeves that zip off for comfort. Good Queen Bess would be amused.

BASIC SILHOUETTES

The first thing to consider when designing your period clothing is that the shape of the garments is quite different than that of the modern silhouette. Modern clothes follow the natural lines of the body and sometimes emphasize them. Men wear form-fitting shirts and jackets with snug-fitting trousers that effectively turn the leg into a slim tube. Women

Modern silhouette

Elizabethan silhouette

wear clinging knit fabric blouses, pants, skirts and dresses
that expose the leg from the knee down, and clearly reveal the
shape of the body from the knee up.

Elizabethan clothing followed the shape of the body only
nominally, at least in the case of the upper classes who were
the fashion setters. In many instances, the style reshaped the
body, or at least, certain selected parts of it. The clothing
of the lower classes followed the lines of the body more sen-
sibly, but that was only to be expected. The lower classes had
to work for a living and their clothes had to be functional,
rather than fashionable. They followed fashion, sort of, by
wearing simplified versions of what had been fashionable 50
years before.

They made their bodies fit the clothes, rather than the
other way around. In the cases where the styles reshaped the
body, the work was done by boning and padding in strategic
places. Upper class ladies wore corsets to flatten and push up
their breasts, bum rolls to pad out their hips and support the
weight of their skirts, and cone-shaped hoop skirts called farthingales to carry the skirts out from the body.

Gentlemen padded the chest, shoulders, and sometimes the sleeves of their doublets, and usually had some boning down the front of them to help them keep the line long and straight. They would also stuff their trunk hose with silk, straw, wool or bran, thereby giving the appearance of walking pillows. They were also not above wearing corsets of their own, or boning the doublet to obtain a fashionably slim figure. Noble children were often put into corsets as soon as they could walk.

Early in the reign, many gentlemen still wore the codpiece, a stuffed and padded bit of male vanity on a level with a modern woman's padded brassiere. The codpiece went out of fashion during this period, never to return. Peasant clothes retained the codpiece as a triangular flap which evolved into the trouser fly in the early 1800's.

English & German man with codpieces

CHOOSING YOUR ALTER EGO

The next thing to think about when designing your period clothing is what type of character you will be portraying. This is of primary importance. You cannot be your twentieth century self in sixteenth century clothing. You will feel more comfortable in your clothes if you have a character to match. And, conversely, if you have a character, you will have an easier

10

time designing the clothes that go with it.

Cost

If you have a choice of what kind of character you are going to be, you should first consider how much money you have to spend on fabric and trim. You could make a simple peasant outfit for less than $50, or spend more than $300 on material, trim and jeweling for a courtier's suit. Average prices will range from $30-$50 for lower class, $50-$150 for middle class, and $150 on up for upper class. These prices are for the cost of materials and trim only. Don't be surprised if the trim costs more than the fabric.

Buying things on sale, recycling fabrics from other sources, finding special bargains can all bring down the cost quite a bit, but you should not expect to get a finished courtier's suit for less than $50.

To cut your costs, shop the remanents tables in fabric stores. Search out mill-end outlets and drop by often. You will find expensive cloth of good quality for much less than you would expect to pay. Fabric with streaky dye jobs, or flaws which don't interfere with the strength of the fabric may be an excellent choice for a peasant costume, because it will look more rustic.

Comfort

After examining your pocketbook, you should next consider the aspect of comfort. Outdoor events in the summer are usually hot, as are stage plays under lights, and the most comfortable people under these circumstances are those with the least amount of cloth on their bodies, that is, the peasants. The higher your social status, the more beautiful you will be and the less comfortable you will be, as well as more restricted in your movements. If you feel you must have a lot of freedom of move- ment in your clothes, you should forget portraying a noble character.

Please remember that children dressed exactly like minia- ture adults and were expected to behave like it. If you are clothing a child, try to remember his or her comfort. If your child is just panting to be a little courtier, make sure that he understands in advance that he may be uncomfortable and severly restricted in his movements and behavior. No climbing trees for him.

Skill

Finally, consider your time and sewing skills before diving into a re-creation, say, of Elizabeth's coronation gown, or the Ermine portrait (a sketch of it is on page 3 of this book). Rate your sewing skills on a range from 1 to 10, 10 being profess- ional level (pattern drafting, draping, tailoring experience, and some practical costuming experience), and 1 being someone who has made simple garments from commercial patterns.

To make a courtier's suit, your skills should be ideally at an 8 or above. It should take a good professional from 40 to 200 hours of work, depending on the detailing (hand finishing, millinery, jeweling, embroidery and so forth). A peasant outfit will take the same person less than a day to complete.

In order to make a lower class person's clothes should require a skill level of 1 or above, because it is much simpler in design and execution, with far fewer details to be added. Middle class clothing will fit somewhere in between, depending on complexity.

Now that we have told you all the scary parts, our advice to you is BE COURAGEOUS! Nothing ventured, nothing gained. If you carefully think out each step and detail in advance, make working sketches every time you have a question, and assemble paper and/or cloth mockups as needed, and be willing to take extra time, you can not only create anything you desire, but you will also teach yourself valuable skills along the way. Patience and a desire to learn are your best tools.

Surprise!

12

Stage Costumes

Most of the costumes we are dealing with in this book are meant to be viewed from conversational distance, not from a proscenium arch. The information contained in this book of course applies to stage costuming as well, but you must keep in mind a few other things when sewing for the stage.

Stage costuming must often fall prey to small budgets and tight schedules. These costumes depend on impact from a distance, rather than tiny, meticulous detailing. Fabrics that would be out of the question for historical re-creations where every detail of construction will be seen, can be terrific on stage. Loud colors become muted under harsh stage lighting, and color combinations that no one could wear on the street can often give the best impact on stage. Patterns were woven not printed on the fabric, but who will know from fifteen feet away whether that stripe is woven or printed on the fabric.

The point of this is that whatever the use you will be putting your Elizabethan clothing to, hard work and creativity will guarantee your success.

Making It Real

Now that you have chosen your class of character, it is time to flesh it out. A human being is more than a flat, cardboard cutout. A person is a multi-dimensional creation with many facets, just like a rare jewel.

Some things to think about are possible occupation, social position within your class of society, and family life. Questions to ask yourself can be the following: Who are your parents and what do they do for a living? How many siblings? Are you married? If so, how many children have you had, living and dead? Remember, families tended to be large, with a high infant mortality rate. What are your ambitions. Do you want to better yourself or do you not care? Do you dress above your station?

Your research will bring out more questions and answers, and you should have fun building your character to go with your clothes, and building your clothes to go with your character.

Elizabethan embroidery motif

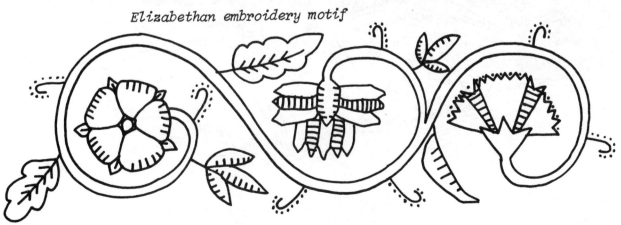

RESEARCH

Which brings us to what can be the most stimulating part of getting ready: research. Your most useful source of information will be the public library. The Dewey Decimal number for English history during Elizabeth's reign is 942.055 and the number for history of Costume is 391. Art books with many useful pictures of a variety of people throughout history may be found under the Dewey Decimal number 791.

These sections of the library are where you will be doing much of your initial research. Later on, if you want, you can expand your activities to include particular topics that interest you. You may find yourself fascinated by period methods of making fabric, or lace. Blackwork embroidery may capture your

imagination, or the religious conflicts which were the source of many wars, including the Spanish Armada. Perhaps you will want to learn all you can about a specific person such as Sir Francis Drake, or Philip II of Spain, or Ivan the Terrible of Russia. El Greco was a contemporary of Elizabeth, as was Ieyasu Tokugawa. And there is always Shakespeare.

Next to costume books, the best sources of pictures of period clothing are art books which are rich in paintings of the appropriate historical period. Many of these are portraits of upper class people wearing their best clothes and therefore are inappropriate for studying the garments of the lower classes. Peasants never had their portraits done, but you can see a lot of working class types around the edges of group scenes, and most paintings by the Flemish Master Breugel have as their central theme, lower class people at work and play.

When building historical clothing for yourself or others, keep in mind what colors are most flattering to the person who will be wearing the clothing. Very few people look good in pure white or pure black. If there are other strong reasons why an unflattering color must be used, then try to mute its effect by adding trim or other detailing, especially near the face, in a more flattering color, to help compensate. Begin observing people and noting what colors look great on what hair and skin coloring, and vice versa.

If the person who is being costumed is tall and stately with strong features, he or she can take strong colors and color contrasts as well as more dramatic detailing which would tend to overwhelm a more petite figure. Smaller folk, or those with softer features, need more delicate color and detailing.

While doing your research generally, try branching out into books that talk about figure types, and how to minimize flaws while maximizing a person's good points. Pick up books on color theory, which will show you how to make the best use of the colors available to this historical period. Do not, however, accept blindly whatever advice is given in these books. Observation and experimentation are your best research tools.

Embroidery motif

SECTION II: MEN'S CLOTHING

MEN'S FASHIONS: AN OVERVIEW

I. Lower Class

A peasant man would wear at least a shift or shirt, and breeches of some kind. He might wear a laced-up or buttoned jerkin (vest) with or without sleeves over this, and some kind of hat with a biggins (coif) underneath to keep his shaggy hair out of his eyes. All but the poorest would have cloth hosen (stockings) and shoes, or if he wore no hosen, he might have bare legs or long breeches similar to pajama pants, cross gartered from ankle to knee. Cross gartered breeches were commonly worn by the lower classes since before the Conquest 500 years before. He would have a cape in cold weather.

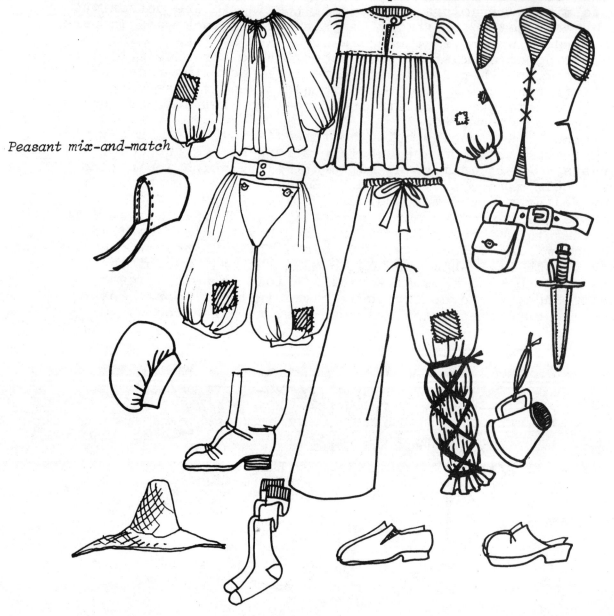

Peasant mix-and-match

Peasant men

At his belt would be a pouch to carry oddments and a small knife for eating purposes. He would be carrying on or about his person, objects pertaining to his profession, whatever it might be. His clothing would probably have dirt and holes or patches on it, and his body was seldom clean, combed or freshly shaven.

Fabrics were coarsely woven, or at least had that appearance. The lower classes mostly spun their own yarn and wove their own cloth, and just because they had to do it does not mean that they were good at it. They wore wool, linen and combinations of the two fibers, such as linsey-woolsey. They also wore leather when they could get it from hunting, and they lined their winter clothes and capes with the skins of rabbits and squirrels.

Colors for dying the fabrics were obtained from vegetable sources available in the vicinity, and consisted of mainly earth colors and muted tones. Blue was done with woad and indigo, yellow with saffron or onion skins, red from madder or cochineal, orange from the safflower, brown from weld. Rust

17

color was gotten by soaking rusting iron in water and green was made by dying yellow over blue. Shifts and shirts were left undyed because they were likely to be washed more often.

Trim on peasant clothes was kept simple and usually consisted of embroidery or plain strips of contrasting fabric sewn to the edges of things to set them off. More often, there was no trim or edge decoration at all.

Since there was seldom enough money or time to buy or make a lot of cloth at one time, the color of one garment hardly ever matched the color of another. Also, since a peasant usually only had one outfit, it didn't get washed very often, so it would be well worn, dirty, and patched. These were working clothes, so not very much time could be given to upkeep.

Worn out clothes were not thrown away, but combined with others and recycled in one form or another until the fibers fell apart. Even then, the remains might have been shredded and carded with fresh wool to fill it out and be rewoven into a whole new piece of fabric.

II. Lower Middle Class

A man of this class would be wearing the same basic garments described in the section on peasants, but they would be somewhat cleaner, neater and less well worn. He would own more than one set of clothes, so they could be cleaned and mended more often.

He would have more than one shirt or shift and might even have a little neck ruffle on the collar. His jerkin or doublet would fit less like a sack and might be made of the same material as his breeches. His hosen would not have great gaping holes in them, but be mended or patched if old, and he definitly owned at least one pair of shoes or boots.

His hair and whiskers would be better trimmed and perhaps recently combed. He would wear a coif with a flat hat or straw hat over that. His hat might sport a feather or two in imitation of his betters.

He would have about him, like the peasant, something pertaining to his profession, as well as the usual belt pouch and eating knife. When the weather was cold, he had a nice warm fur trimmed cape, or maybe the whole cape would be fur lined,with a contrasting fur trim.

The fabrics of his clothes were less coarse than the peasant's rough woven stuff, but they were still highly textured. They were sometimes purchased from professional weavers, so would be finer and more closely woven. They were still mostly made of wool and linen, plus the usual blends, but this does not mean that the cloth all looked alike. There was a great variety in textural and color contrasts, and the possible combinations were almost endless.

Colors of fabrics might be more intense than for peasants, but the nature of the vegetable dyestuffs was such that colors would still be fairly subdued. And they all faded with time and washing. Servants and apprentices were usually dressed in indigo blue clothing because it was a cheap and plentiful dye,

so anybody with pretentions to social standing would avoid that color. The darkest and most intense colors were for formal wear, even back then, but true black was a difficult color to obtain and maintain, and therefore was restricted to the well to do people who had the money to spare for formal clothes.

Trims were simple. Plain colored bands, such as ribbon or rows of embroidery were used on the edges of garments to set them off. These were always colored, never gold or silver metallic threads or trim because of the cost and the sumptuary laws. A person of this class would not wear lace. Hand made lace (and that was the only kind) was prohibitivly expensive.

If any jewelry was worn, it would be very simple in design, consisting of glass or flat cut semi-precious stones in settings of brass or pewter. Pins would be the most common type of ornament, with buttons also made as ornaments rather than just plain fastenings. Non-functional jewelry was for the upper classes.

III. Upper Middle Class

The upper middle class man would quite often be gentry or petty nobility, with his own house and lands. He might also be a high-ranking servant in a nobleman's household, a rich merchant or highly skilled craftsman of some kind. He would have his own servants, among whom would be a valet, a personal body servant whose sole task was to see to his master's clothing and personal appearance. Therefore, the upper middle class man would dress quite well, if he could afford it. He might choose to pay the sumptuary tax on some item of his apparel so that he could be even more richly dressed.

His shirts were made of fine linen or cotton with neck and wrist ruffles, and perhaps a touch of blackwork embroidery on the collar and cuffs or edging the ruffles. Or he might have some lace on it if he could afford it.

Over the shirt, he wore a close-fitting doublet with long or short skirting that ended somewhere between his upper thigh and the knee, depending on his age and respectability. He wore breeches or slops, also called trunk-hose or upper-stocks on his lower half and they were decorated to some degree.

His hosen, also called nether-stocks now reached all the way up his legs and were sometimes knitted instead of sewn from bias cut fabric, as was most commonly done. Knitted hosen, however, were fabulously expensive, because they were always hand knitted, usually out of silk, and cost upwards of five pounds a pair. That was a princely sum for those days, perhaps equivalent to $200 nowadays. That's a lot to pay for pantyhose, even silk ones! His fine shoes were decorated with buckles or ribbon shoe-roses and his garter ties were sometimes embroidered or fringed on the ends.

He wore either a flat cap or a tall crowned, small brimmed hat with feathers and a fancy hatband. His hair was worn short and older men and conservative types covered their heads with a coif or biggins under their hats. Men of this class were likely to go clean shaven, or if they had whiskers, they were well trimmed.

Many of the older or more conservative gentlemen wore knee-length coats called Schaubes, after the German, or if worn long, were called Gowns. These coats were worn over doublets and slops as an outer garment, instead of a cape. The Schaubes resembled modern choir robes with a deep collar and revers of black velvet or fur. For winter wear, outer garments would be completely lined with fur.

Pouch and dagger hung from his belt and he might have a fine gold chain around his neck to denote wealth, rank or position. His clothes were trimmed, embroidered, and jeweled as much as he could afford, and the sumptuary laws would allow, and his appearance was sometimes little different from that of a noble gentleman.

Fabrics were still the practical wool and linen, but they were much finer quality than before. Added to this were cottons for undergarments, and silk satins and velvets in modest quantities. Those who could afford to dress especially well were always skirting the edges of the sumptuary laws, trying to get away with just a little bit more than their neighbors.

Colors were brighter jewel tones, but not in shocking shades and black was the color for the most formal of occasions.

Trim was more ornate, but still mostly restricted to geometric
forms or bands of plain colored embroidery or ribbon. The rich-
est paid their sumptuary taxes and wore gold and silver trim,
and were richly decorated, beaded, pearled, or bejeweled, just
like the nobles.

IV. Upper Class & Nobility

The Nobleman was the peacock and fashion setter of the land.
He had money, property and titles. He wielded all the politi-
cal power in England, although he needed help to get dressed.
Without his personal servant, he was helpless.

Many noblemen wore their fortunes on their backs, quite
literally, with clothing heavily pearled, jeweled and embroidered. The courtier had to make a brave show to attract the
attention of the spinster Queen. Her favor would more than make
up for the sometimes ruinous expense, as she dispensed valuable
monopolies to her favorites. If a gentleman could impress the
Queen and keep her favor, his fortune was made. So his clothes
had to be ornate.

His shirt was made of fine linen, cotton, or silk, with
lace-edged neck and wrist ruffs. If he wore a very large ruff,
it was separate from the shirt. A smaller ruff would be sewn to
the shirt as part of the collar. It might be stitched with blackwork embroidery with gold thread accents and had fine ribbon
ties with gold or silver tips on them. If he was pot-bellied or
stout, he probably wore a corset to give himself a more slender
waistline.

His doublet was close fitting and might have either a peascod belly (after 1575), or perhaps a more natural line down the
front. The waist was pointed at the center front and had a short
skirting or tabs at the bottom. The shoulders had epaulets or
wings, padded rolls, or tabs to make the shoulders look wider

21

and also to help conceal the points that tied the sleeves on. His sleeves would be very ornate and usually, but not always matched the fabric of the doublet. A noble gentleman might wear a sleeveless jerkin over his doublet, fastening it only at the bottom to create a V-shape in front, further slenderizing his waistline.

Below the waist, he wore slops that came to mid-thigh, padded Venetian breeches that reached the knees, or he wore pansied slops which were little more than a padded hip roll over cannions, a kind of tight-fitting knee length pair of breeches. Pansied slops showed off the legs and buttocks to advantage if the man had a good figure. It was an age of appreciation of men's legs.

His hosen were hand knitted of the finest silk and cost upwards of five pounds a pair. His garters were tied or buckled and were embroidered with gold or silver thread. His court shoes were made of velvet or soft leather, beautifully decorated with jeweled buckles or shoe roses.

His hair was short and whiskers, if any, were neatly trimmed and pomaded. His hat might be a flat cap, or a high crowned, narrow brimmed creation. Small fortunes were lavished on the decoration of the hatband. He spent slightly less on the feathers that were pinned into the hatband.

His cape was heavily decorated and quite often lined with the fur of some rare animal. He would have a pouch, sword and dagger hanging from his belt, and the dandy would also carry a pomander and fan. The nobleman often wore gloves, and they were scented and embroidered as well

If the gentleman had any money left after clothing himself, he spent the remainder on jewelry to adorn his person. Many courtiers wore a pear-shaped pearl in one pierced ear. Hands glittered with rings and gloves were often slit at the knuckle to better display them. They wore gold chains, and jeweled buttons and brooches. They glistened and gleamed like stars in the sky and were the light of the Queen's court.

When he rode to the hunt, the courtier wore a leather doublet or sleeveless jerkin over his shirt; sturdy fabric or leather breeches; and leather riding boots and gloves. Capes were tied on behind the saddle in case of bad weather, but they were seldom needed unless it rained. The vigorous activity was sufficent to keep the rider quite warm enough.

Fabrics were glorious. Cost was no object and skilled weavers could seemingly work miracles. Velvet could have as many as five seperate heights in the weave and some designs took on a three-dimensional look. The weavers of the Renaissance could produce cloth with their simple looms, tools and immense patience that modern computer-run looms cannot duplicate. Silks, satins, damask brocades and velvets were in great demand, along with the usual wools, linens, and a small amount of fine Indian and Egyptian cotton. Fabrics for everyday wear or hunting were less fancy and more practical than cerimonial garb. Most garments were decorated with edging of gold or silver embroidery, richly beaded and bejeweled. Small objects, such as hats, purses, nightcaps, partlet or shirt collar and cuffs, as well as handkerchiefs were heavily stitched with bright silks and metallic threads of precious metal.

Colors were brilliant, but not loud. Black was still most proper for formal wear, but it was a difficult color to achieve and maintain, as it was not color-fast and the color needed renewing often. Early in her reign, Elizabeth preferred a shade of orangey-gold called Tawney, but later in her life, she preferred virginal white for herself and the ladies closest to her.

An important fact to keep in mind is that all their lovely colors came from vegetable or mineral sources, and as such, the intensity of hue available to them was much less than modern dyes. To estimate what their dyes were like, think more in terms of the tones found in the hearts of jewels.

The men and women of Gloriana's court could afford to dress as they liked, so long as no one tried to out-shine the Queen. She reserved for herself the right to outdress them all for her own pleasure.

SHIRTS

Shirts were worn by all men of all classes. The fabric they were made from, and the complexity of the designs were dependent on the man's station in life and the work he did..

One kind of shirt for a peasant man looked exactly like a woman's high-necked drawstring shift or chemise. If you want to make that kind of shirt, we suggest that you consult the instructions for making the shift in the women's clothing section. We have also experimented with the chemise type shirt based on the clown-suit pattern as a shirt for men. While it is not as historically accurate as the others, it is easy to make, and fits well under doublets. Consult the women's section for directions on this shirt as well.

A great men's peasant or farmer's shirt already exists as a commercial pattern. Folkwear pattern #102, the French Cheese-maker's Smock is a wonderful, traditional peasant shirt and is ideal as it is, with no alterations necessary.

The other two main designs for men's shirts are described here below. As you can see from the picture, the main difference between the two shirt styles is that the first type has the fabric of the body of the shirt gathered into a yoke, and the second type has a straight body type, with no yoke. They each have their advantages and disadvantages, and are both historically proper. Either shirt might have no collar, a flat collar, or a standing collar. For the higher classes, the shirt would have neck and wrist ruffs attached to the standing collar and cuffs. These shirts always had long, full sleeves gathered into cuffs which tied or buttoned, and the neck was usually tied shut, too, with "bandstrings".

Yoke shirt

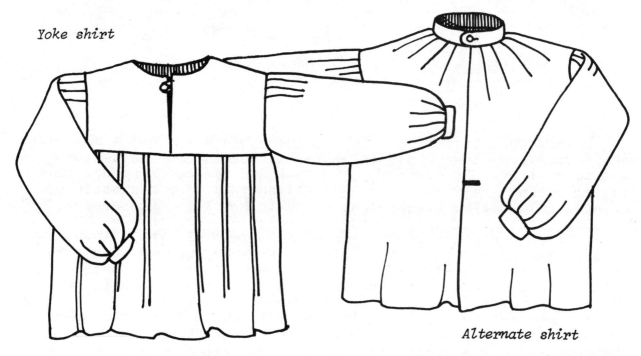

Alternate shirt

24

To make any of these shirts, we strongly suggest that you use a 100% cotton (muslin) or other natural fiber for comfort's sake, for a very simple reason. Natural fibers breathe. Polyester and poly-blend fibers do not. This may not seem very important to you until the mercury hits 90 degrees in the shade, if you could find any, or the stage lights are toasting you well done. But then it will be vitally important to your health and comfort to have something that you can sweat into, that will carry the moisture away from your skin, instead of insulating you like artificial fibers do.

Yoke Shirt

In order to make the shirt with a yoke, you will need a man's regular shirt pattern of the correct size. See the pattern section for a picture of the suggested shirt type to help you in selecting the right pattern. Your shirt will need only the pattern pieces illustrated here. Remove them from the rest and stuff the remaining pieces back into the envelope so you won't lose them. You might need them someday. So far, so good.

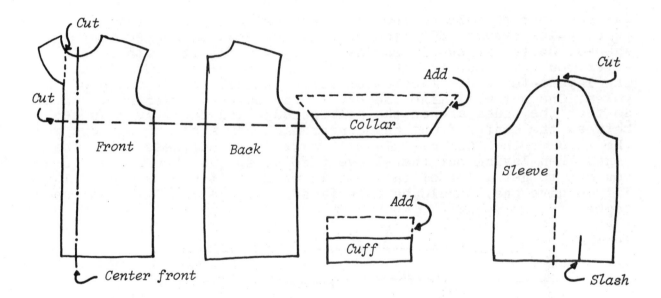

Take the front pattern piece and draw a horizontal line all the way across it 8"-10" down from the top of the center front. Now, draw another horizontal line 10"-12" down from the center back on the back piece. Cut your pattern pieces along these lines. These pieces are your yoke pattern. Add 1" to the top edges of the pieces you cut off and those will be the pattern for the body of the shirt. The sleeve pattern piece should be cut in half lengthwise and spread to widen it, and the cuffs should also be cut a little wider.

For a flat collar, called a falling band, use the collar piece that came with the shirt and extend it several inches to give it a more period look.

For a standing collar, either cut the corners off of the collar piece you have, or design one that will fit better. To do that, cut a pattern piece out of plain paper 5" wide and your neck measurement plus 3" long. The bottom of the collar piece should curve a little so that the collar will fit into the neck opening better, and the back should be a little higher in the back than in the front. This will look better, even if it sounds harder, and will prevent you from choking yourself when you lower your chin.

High collars

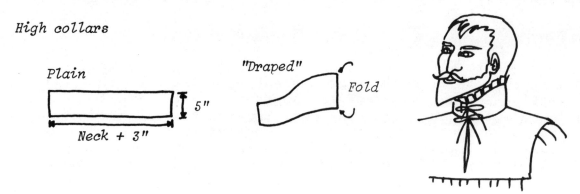

Lay out your pattern on the cloth approximately like the picture, which assumes 36" wide muslin fabric which has been prewashed. Better it should shrink before you cut it, rather than after you have made the shirt and washed it afterwards. Adjust the layout for wider fabrics or larger sizes. Cut two sets of yokes. One set will line the other. Lay out the lower body pieces so that the sides are on the selvage edge and there is a space between the center front and center back edges of the pattern and the fold of the fabric. This will make extra fullness below the yoke. When laying out the sleeve pieces, spread them as far as you can to get a lot of fullness in them. Cuff pieces and collar, if you have one, should be interfaced, but the yoke will not need to be.

Fabric layout

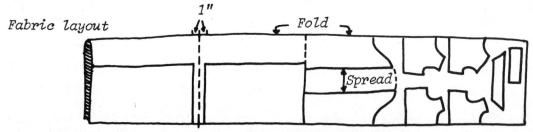

Slash the end of the sleeve pieces to 3" up from the edge and halfway toward the back of the sleeve from the underarm seam. Turn under the edges of the slashed part twice and sew. Do the same for the other sleeve.
1. Sew together the front and back yoke pieces at the shoulder seams. Do it again for the yoke lining. Gather or pleat the lower body pieces onto the yoke pieces. 2. Then gather or pleat the sleeves into the armholes. 3. Sew up the shirt side seams from the sleeve end to the armpit, then from there to the hem.

4. Now, gather or pleat the sleeves into the cuffs, and finish the cuffs with invisible flat hooks & eyes, buttons and button loops, or ribbon ties.

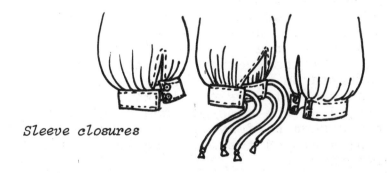

Sleeve closures

For a shirt with no collar, take the yoke lining and lay it over the yoke with right sides together. Sew up one side of the neckline, around the neck, and back down the other side. Clip the curves and turn the lining to the inside. Press under the remaining edges of the lining ½" and sew by hand or machine. Finish off the top of the neck with a button and button loop, hidden hook & eye, or ribbon ties.

5. For a shirt with a flat or standing collar, the collar is finished and sewn into the neck opening before the yoke lining is applied. The lining is then attached as above. If built-in neck and wrist ruffs are desired on the high-necked shirt, sew a double row of box-pleated lace or self fabric to the edges of the collar and cuffs. This is best done before sewing the two collar pieces or cuff pieces together. Hem the shirt and it is finished.

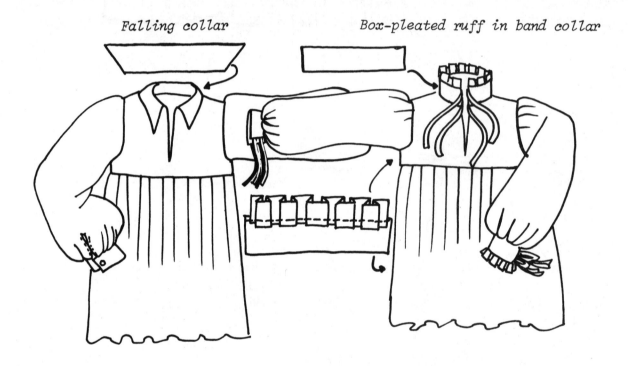

Falling collar

Box-pleated ruff in band collar

Alternate Shirt

For the other kind of shirt, you will need less fabric and will not be cutting the pattern apart as for the first type. Lay out the pattern pieces as shown. The sleeves should be kept very full, but there will be less fabric in the body of the shirt. The neck is cut larger and will need to be gathered slightly into the collar, if you want one; or a simple collar band, if you don't. All the collar and cuff instructions are the same.

This shirt is based on a picture of an actual 16th century man's shirt. It had several rows of blackwork embroidery down the front of the shirt, down the sleeves, and on the collar and cuffs of the shirt. It was sewn halfway up the front and had a placket behind the ties which closed the neck opening. The cuffs also were fastened with ties.

28

This kind of shirt might be better worn under a tight-fitting doublet, where you would want less bulk in the body section. Since this style is a little more restrictive than the other type, it would be worn more by nobles, than by the working classes.

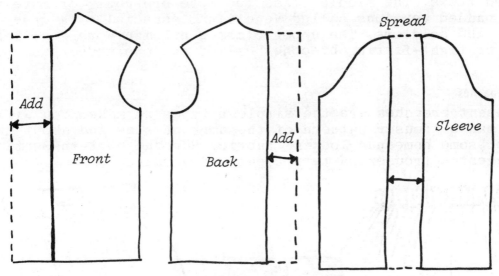

Alternate shirt pattern

Illustration of 16th century shirt with blackwork embroidery

29

BREECHES

Breeches were worn in one form or another by men of all classes. The peasant wore baggy, knee-length breeches, or cross gartered trews. The middle class men wore breeches, or more tailored, padded versions called Venetians, especially favored by sailors and soldiers. The upper class gentleman wore Venetians, slops, or tight-fitting breeches called canions under pansied slops.

Peasant Breeches

Peasant breeches are the simplest types to make. You will need a man's trouser pattern of the correct size and about two yards of some homespun looking fabric. See the pattern section for suggested trouser pattern types and yardages.

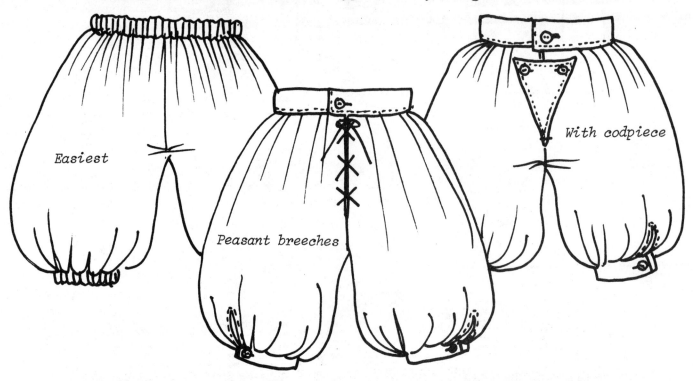

Easiest

Peasant breeches

With codpiece

Measure the man from his waist to just above or below his knee, depending on how long you want them to be. Add 4"-6" to this measurement. Measure that distance down from the waist of the pants pattern pieces and cut off the legs at that point. If you want to reuse the pattern, just fold the legs up instead of cutting them off. If you want to have a waistband and legbands, which will look better and be more authentic, cut one paper pattern piece 8" wide and your waist measurement plus 3" long. Cut another pattern piece 4" wide and the leg measurement (above or below the knee) plus 2" long for the legband. Cut two triangles 8" across the top and 12"-14" from top edge to point. This will be the optional codpiece.

Lay out the pattern pieces as illustrated. Cut only one waistband and two legbands, if you are going to use them.

30

Sew the crotch seams, leaving the front seam open enough to put in your fasteners later. We suggest you use hooks and eyes or grommets for lacing. Now fold and sew the inside leg seams. For the simplest pants, turn the waist and leg edges twice for casings and insert elastic. If you are using elastic in the waistband, sew up the crotch seam all the way, before turning the top edge down.

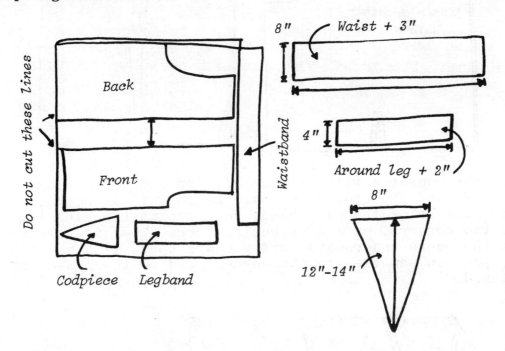

If you are using a waistband and legbands, rather than elastic, slash each leg vertically up to 4" from the bottom edge of the leg piece, halfway between the two inside leg seams. Turn and sew the slashings toward the inside. Now pleat or gather the top edge of the breeches into the waistband and finish off with flat hooks & eyes, buttons, or grommets. Then do the same for the bottom edges and the legbands.

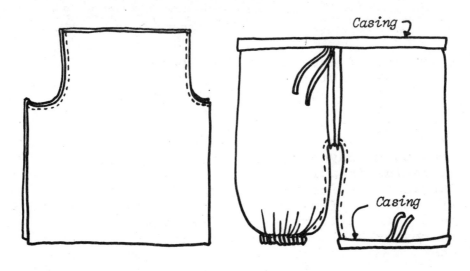

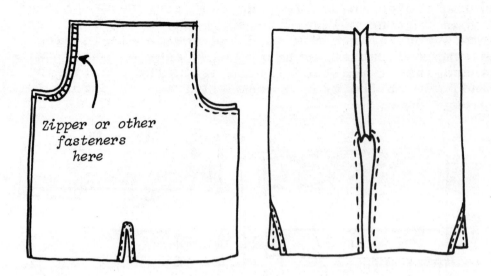

Line the codpiece with self fabric and sew the bottom point at the bottom of the crotch so that the top of the codpiece comes to just below the waistband. Work two buttonholes into the top two corners, or sew on button loops. Then sew two buttons to the pants underneath, and you are done. If you would rather, you can sew ties to the corners and to the pants and tie them closed.

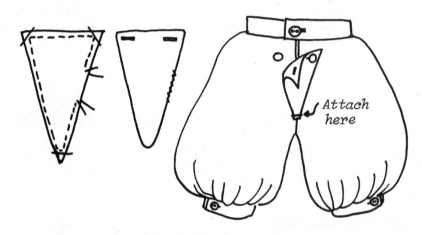

Trews

Another version of breeches called trews can be made with a drawstring or pajama pants pattern. Trews had been worn since Saxon times and before. Just make the pattern out of a rustic looking cloth and cross-garter them below the knees after they are put on. Use leather thongs or twisted strips of cloth to cross-garter them. These pants should be worn by only the very poorest of peasants. Anyone with a little ambition would try to look a bit more fashionable.

Fabric appropriate for these types of breeches would be only the roughest, coarsest fabrics. Linen, loosely woven woolens and cottons should work well. Stay away from any fabric with nap, such as corduroy or brushed denim, or fabric with a sheen, like a chino blend.

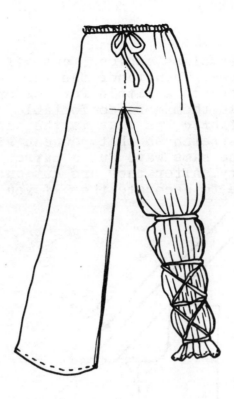

Venetians

The pattern for the Venetian breeches is only a little different than the peasant breeches, being fuller at the top and less full at the bottom. Use the waistband and legband pieces, as they will make the breeches look much better than elastic with casings. Leave off the codpiece altogether.

For these pants, use a nicer fabric like a waled or no-wale corduroy, or a brushed denim. Follow the construction details for the peasant breeches, omitting the parts about elastic casings and the codpiece.

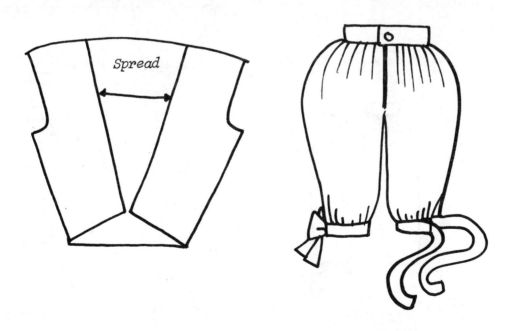

Canions

To make the upper class canions, cut off or fold the pattern up just above the knee. Then taper the legs, so they will fit snugly, and extend crotch a little for comfort. Trust us. It really will help make them more comfortable. Lay out the pattern on the bias of the fabric, as that is the only way to give such tight pants enough stretch so that you can sit down. Remember to cut the lining the same way. Cut a narrow waistband, but legbands are unnecessary. After they are cut out, but before they are sewn is the time to decorate them if you want.

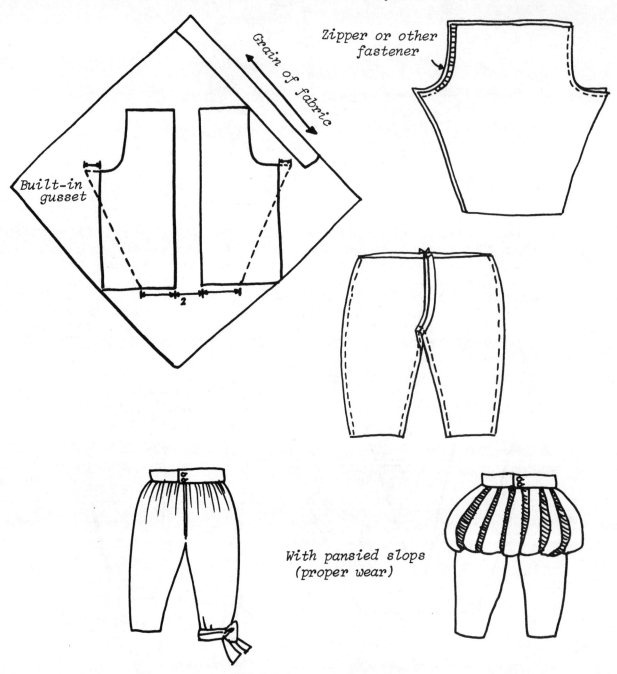

Grain of fabric

Built-in gusset

2

Zipper or other fastener

With pansied slops (proper wear)

Sew the crotch seams, leaving the front seam open enough to
put in hooks, grommets, or an invisible zipper. Now, sew the
inside leg seams. Without turning the canions right side out,
try the pants on the gentleman you are making them for. Pin them
tighter, if necessary, after making sure that he can still sit
down and make the alterations, if any are needed. Now, make the
lining the same way and sew it into the canions. Then, ease the
top edge onto the waistband and finish with hooks, buttons, or
grommets. Remember that gentlemen only wore canions under pansied slops and never by themselves. Directions for the pansied
slops will follow in the next section.

Venetian breeches &
pansied slops with canions

35

TRUNKHOSE OR SLOPS

Trunk-hose, also called galligaskins, or more commonly, slops, were worn by middle and upper class men. They differed from bree-ches in that they had panes, or strips of contrasting material laid over the fabric of the short inner breeches. Slops were ev-ery length, from upper to mid thigh, and sometimes to the knee, and were usually stuffed with something to make them stand out, like straw, wool, bran, silk, or captured enemy flags.

To make slops, you will need the man's pants pattern of the correct size. Check the yardage section for yardage requirements. Slops look best when made with good quality, medium weight fab-rics. The panes can be made of wool, velveteen, corduroy, brushed denim, or appropriate blend. The lining can be a lighter weight fabric, the type to be determined by the social position and wealth of the character.

Measure the man from the waist to where you want the slops to end, and add 4". Cut off or fold up the legs of the pattern at this point. Measure the waist, divide by 14 and add 1½". This will be the width of each of the 14 panes of the slops. Make the length of the panes the same as that of the pants pat-tern pieces. Make two pattern pieces as illustrated, using the tissue pattern to duplicate the front and back crotch curves. These pieces will fill in the inner leg, where the panes do not go. For the contrasting lining, spread the two halves of the leg

36

pieces so that they are at least 12" apart at the bottom, but still touching at the top, and draw a curve from one bottom corner to the other. For the inner lining, fold the pattern pieces so that the leg will fit snugly, but not too tightly for comfort, and fold up the bottoms 3".

Cut a waistband pattern 8" wide and the waist measurement plus 3" long, and a legband pattern 4" wide and the thigh measurement plus 2" long. If you lack confidence, make the inner lining out of a cheap fabric. Attach the waist and legbands, and try this mocked-up garment on the gentleman who will be wearing it when it is finished. Have him move around and sit down to make sure that it won't bind.

Cut 14 panes for the slops out of the fabric you will be using. Do the same for the lining, and heavy interfacing. Cut the filler panes out of the fabric and lining, but omit the interfacing for these pieces. The crotch area will feel funny if it has stiffening in it. Cut out the contrasting outer lining, then use a sturdy fabric to cut the inner lining, which will not show when the slops are finished. Finally, cut out the waistband and legbands out of the pane fabric. The waistband, but not the legbands should be interfaced.

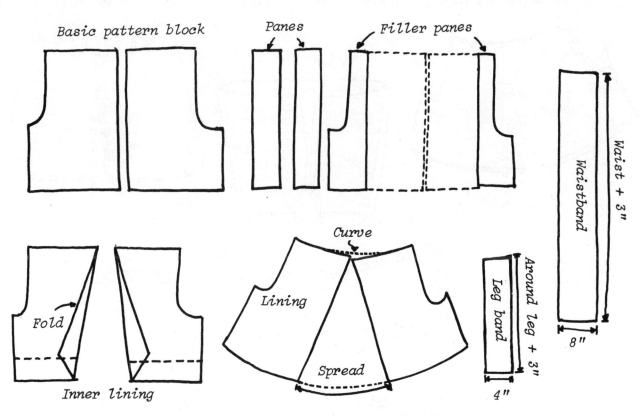

Sew the pane pieces to the pane lining and interfacing. Turn and press each pane. Decorate them at this stage, except for jeweling or beading, because it will be much harder later on. Lay seven of the finished panes on one of the cut pieces of outer lining. Lay one of the filler panes at each end. The panes should just about fit across the top edge, and spread out at the

37

bottom. Overlap the panes slightly, if necessary, to make them fit across the top. Pin, then stitch, to hold the panes in place. Repeat for the other leg.

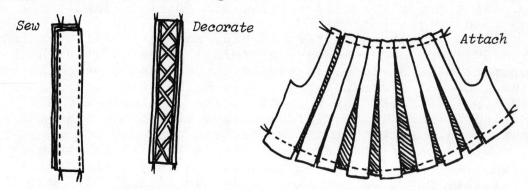

Sew the crotch seam, leaving an opening for an invisible zipper, hooks, ties, or grommets. Sew the inner leg seams. Then sew the inner lining seams, leaving the front seam open to sew to the other opening later, before the fasteners are put in.

Pleat the legs of the slops onto one edge of the legbands and sew the bottom of the inner lining to the other edge. Fold the legbands in half, so the inner lining is inside, and stitch.

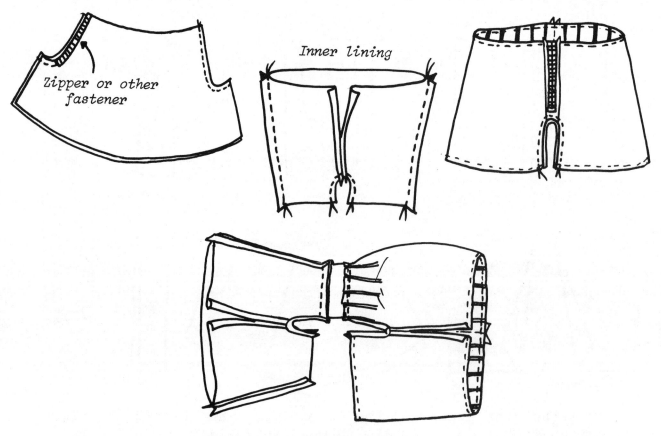

If you want the slops to keep their pumpkin-like shape, now is the time to stuff them. We suggest that you use nylon net, because it is inexpensive, lightweight, lets air pass through, and is washable and dry cleanable. Stuff the slops loosely, be-

38

tween the outer and inner lining, until you think it is full enough. Then, pull up the inner lining until the top of the inner lining meets the top edge of the slops. Since the inner lining is a little shorter than the slops, this should make them puff out a little, even without stuffing. That's all right. They're supposed to do that.

We have found that the nylon net packs down, after awhile, and the slops will need to be fluffed, like a pillow, every so often. With time, and many wearings, even fluffing them up may not work. You will then have to open up the back part of the waistband, and add to the stuffing. Keep this in mind, when sewing the waistband on, so you don't over-reinforce it.

Now, sew the inner lining to the top of the slops and add the waistband. Sew flat hooks and eyes to the waistband, add the fasteners of your choice on the front, and you are done, at last. *Whew*

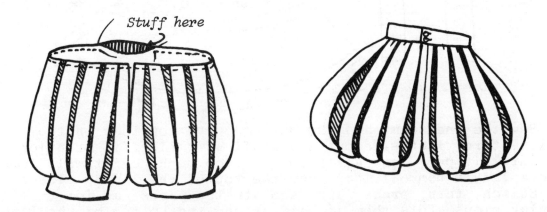

Another type of waistband is pointed in the front, and its advantage over the easier, straight waistband is that it allows the snug, long-waisted doublet to fit more smoothly over it. Below is a sketch of the pattern piece. Make a mock-up out of cheap fabric until you are sure you have it the way you want it, then cut your fabric and interfacing. Sew it together along the top edge and fronts, as shown. Turn and press. Ease the slops into it and sew in place, making allowances for the longer front. Finish as with the other style.

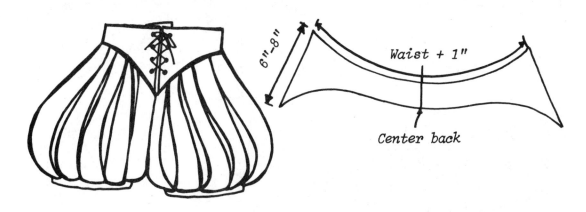

Pansied Slops

Pansied slops are much easier to make, but must be worn over canions (see breeches). Cut the panes, pane lining, and interfacing as before. Also cut whichever waistband you want, and interface that. For the contrasting lining, cut a long, shallow curved piece, which is half as wide as your panes are long. The top edge of the curved piece should be 8"-12" longer than your waist measurement, and the bottom edge should be that much longer than you hip measurement. Cut a lining for the curved piece, which might be the same fabric or different.

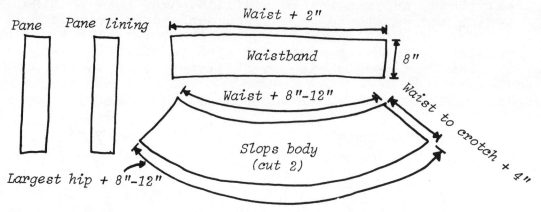

Pane   Pane lining

Waist + 2"

Waistband   8"

Waist + 8"-12"

Waist to crotch + 4"

Slops body
(cut 2)

Largest hip + 8"-12"

Sew the end seams and the bottom curve together on the lining, turn right side out and stuff with fiberfil or nylon net until it puffs out a little. Not too much, or it will look like a lady's bumroll. Now, sew the top of the lining closed.

Stitch, turn, press, and decorate the panes, as for the regular slops. Fold them in half around the bottom of the lining so that the ends of the panes all meet along the top edge. Sew them all together to the lining and add the waistband. You will have to ease the slops into the waistband, because you made the slops big enough to fit over the hips. Finally, sew flat hooks and eyes all down the front to close it and you are done with the pansied slops.

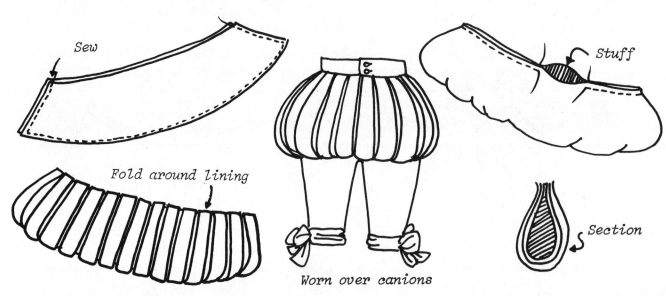

Sew

Stuff

Fold around lining

Section

Worn over canions

40

Cod Pieces

The codpiece had gone out of fashion by the 1580's. Up to that point, it was still seen on some men, so we feel that it should be mentioned here. The first codpieces were seen late in the previous century, but trace their roots to when the men's tunics, or "pourpoints" came into fashion in the mid 1300's. These tunics were so short, that hosen had to come all the way up the leg, and a triangular flap was used to cover what the two legs of the hosen did not. When men began wearing breeches, it seemed natural to transfer the flap to the front of them for convenience.

Some sources theorize that as plate armor evolved and became more sophisticated, the codpiece developed from the cup which protected the man's private parts. There is a good chance that both may be correct, with the hosen version providing the function and reason for development, and the armor version providing the shape.

In the section on breeches, we showed a rudimentary triangular codpiece. What follows, is an assortment of patterns for you to experiment with. These are close to actual codpieces of the period, and can be used to add more realism to breeches or slops. They are not appropriate to Venetian breeches, canions, or pansied slops, for these developed as fashions while the codpiece was going out of fashion.

The codpieces you make can be functional, or merely decorative. It depends on how daring the wearer is. Some men like the convenience, and others don't trust them to stay closed. We have seen both kinds, and usually one can't tell unless the gentleman feels like saying so.

Whichever kind you decide on, make sure that it positioned correctly. It should also be neither too small or too large, unless it is needed to be either way for theatrical reasons. Attach it on the bottom by sewing it on, and fasten it on the top with points (ties), or buttons, which tend to be more secure than ties.

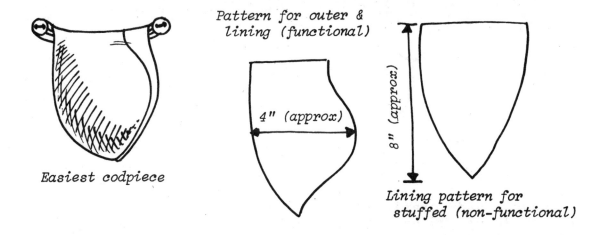

Easiest codpiece

Pattern for outer &
lining (functional)

4" (approx)

8" (approx)

Lining pattern for
stuffed (non-functional)

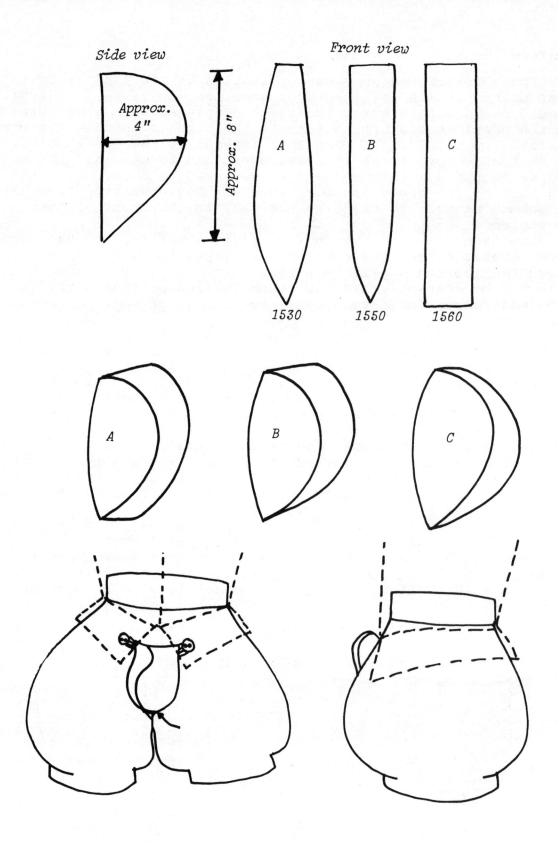

Side view

Front view

Approx. 4"

Approx. 8"

A

B

C

1530

1550

1560

A

B

C

Have fun decorating it with slashes, beading, jeweling, trim, or embroidery. We have seen codpieces lined with fur, but that seems a bit much!

JERKINS

The jerkin can be a shapeless vest worn by the lowest peasant, or it can be a form-fitting, heavily bejeweled garment, differing from a doublet. only in its lack of sleeves. We give directions for lower class jerkins only, because the middle and upper class jerkins were made exactly like doublets without sleeves. Doublet instructions will follow in the next section.

Lower, middle and upper class jerkins

Peasant Jerkin

The simplest peasant jerkin can be made by lengthening a loose-fitting vest pattern. Or it can be made without a pattern by using the following instructions.

Start with a rough, homespun looking kind of fabric. Check the yardage section to see how much you will need. Cut the piece of fabric in half lengthwise, and then cut one of the halves in half again, lengthwise. Fold the piece you didn't cut, in half lengthwise and cut a shallow curve in one end, starting at the fold, down to about 4"-5" away from the fold. This is the back piece. Lay the two smaller pieces on top of each other and make a slanting cut from one end 4"-5" from the edge, to the edge 12" further down. These are the front pieces.

Sew the front pieces to the back piece at the shoulders, so the ends of the back curve meet the ends of the slanted cuts. Then sew the sides together from 12" down from the shoulder seams, to the bottom hem. Turn under all the raw edges of the fabric, if you want to, and wear the jerkin, belted or not, over a peasant shirt and breeches. Keep in mind, that leather was a very common material for jerkins, but don't use any naugahide for it, or you will roast in your own juices. It doesn't breathe the way real leather does.

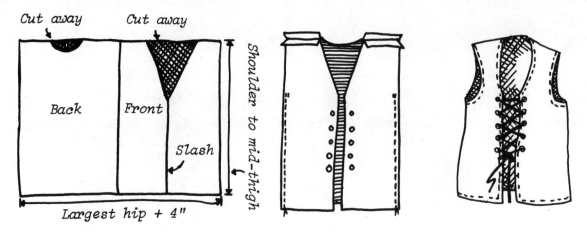

Form-fitting Jerkin

If you want to make a form fitting leather jerkin, we have some suggestions to help you to make it more easily. First, read the section on draping, most particularly, the part that tells how to make a form fitting pattern by wrapping the foot (or body) in tape, after putting on a sock (or T-shirt). This finished body cast should be cut carefully off along where you want the seam lines to be. For a better fit and more ease of movement, you might wish to create extra seams. Squash the pieces flat and make your pattern from these. Do not add a seam allowance. When you have cut your pattern out of the leather, punch rows of parallel holes, and simply lace the jerkin together. You will have a perfect fit.

Leather jerkins were decorated with pinks (punched holes) and slashes (little ones). Look at the old pictures for ideas and suggested patterns to follow.

DOUBLETS

The doublet in one form or another, was the suit coat worn by middle and upper class men. If a man's station in life went up, his doublet tended to fit more closely, until, in the highest ranking men, it was so snug, it sometimes limited free movement. It was usually cut narrower across the back to force the posture straighter. The doublet had epaulets on the shoulders to broaden them and help conceal where the sleeves were tied in. A gentleman might keep the same basic doublet for years, and change its look periodically with new sleeves. Or the sleeves might be sewn in and simply replaced with new ones as necessary. The doublet usually came to a point in front with some kind of skirting attached, either plain or cut into tabs, called picadils.

Plain and Peascod belly doublets

Directions will be shown for a simple, middle class doublet, with variations, and a tight-fitting courtier's doublet, with and without a peascod belly. This is a garment that requires a muslin mock-up for fitting, even for those who feel like they know it all. We don't know it all. We make mock-ups.

Basic Doublet

To make the middle class doublet, including sleeves and epaulets, you will need a man's french-cut or tapered shirt pattern of the correct size. For those who don't know the difference between a french-cut and a regular shirt pattern, see the illustrations in the pattern section. For yardages, see the yardage section.

The doublet may match the fabric of the slops or breeches, but it doesn't have to. It should be a sturdy, nice looking, solid color material, such as brushed denim, wool, waled or waleless corduroy. The lining should be the kind of fabric you can sweat into. Prewash all the fabrics before you cut them, so that they will do their shrinking before they are on your body.

Measure the man from the armpit of his regular shirt, down to where he says his waist is. Add 1" and mark the back pattern piece at this point. Cut across, or fold up the pattern back so that it is that length. Mark the front pattern piece at this point and draw a horizontal line from the side seam to the center front. Mark the center front 3"-4" down from the horizontal line you drew, and draw a slanting line from that point to the waist at the side seam. Cut or fold up the pattern along the slanting line. This line will look better if it is drawn as a curve, rather than a straight line.

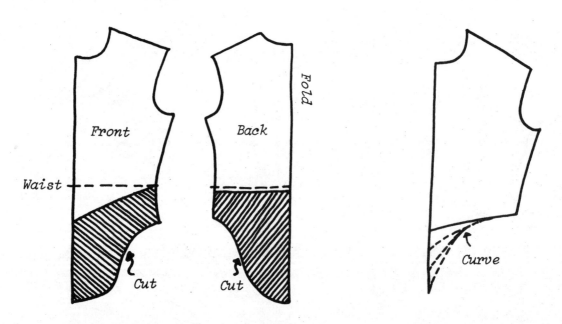

For the skirting, draw a long, shallow curve on a large piece of paper. Now straighten the curve at both ends. Then, draw a parallel line about 6" below the first one, tapering it just a little as you near the ends, so that the ends are 5" wide instead of the 6" at the center. The measurement of the top edge should be the same as the waist of the pattern, and the lower edge should be 4"-6" larger than the hip measurement. If the hips are bigger, make a deeper curve to compensate. The two halves of the pattern must match. You might wish to fold the paper in half and only draw half of the curve, cut it and have a symmetrical curve. If you made a mistake, try again. Paper is cheaper than fabric. The skirting can be left plain or cut into tabs (picadils).

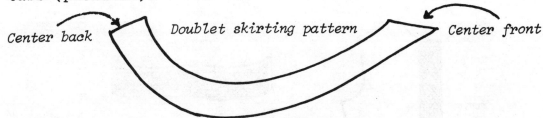

Center back   Doublet skirting pattern   Center front

For the epaulets, cut a pattern piece like an ellipse or oval, with pointed ends, about 18" long from point to point, and about 5" wide at the middle. The epaulets may be left plain, decorated, split, or cut into tabs.

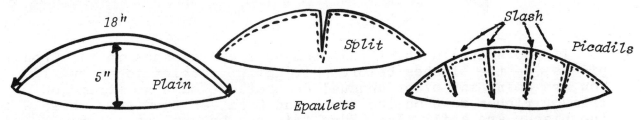

18"

5"   Plain   Split   Slash   Picadils

Epaulets

For the standing collar, cut a pattern piece 5"-6" wide, and the neck measurement plus 3" long. The bottom of the collar piece should curve a little, so that the collar will fit into the neck opening better, and will be higher in the back than the front. This will look better and will keep you from choking yourself on your high, stiff collar, when you lower your chin. Alternatively, you may use the pattern for the draped collar, which will fit your neck almost as well as your skin.

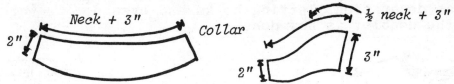

Neck + 3"   Collar   ½ neck + 3"

2"   2"   3"

Lay out the pattern on your fabric, remembering to check to see if the fabric has any nap. Velveteens, corduroys, and brushed denims all have a nap. If the fabric has a nap, be sure that the pattern pieces all face in the same direction. Now, cut the doublet out of the fabric and lining.

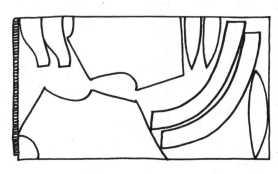

47

Interface a 2" strip on either side of the center front, as well as the epaulets and standing collar. Sew and decorate the collar, epaulets, and skirting separatley, and sew them in later.

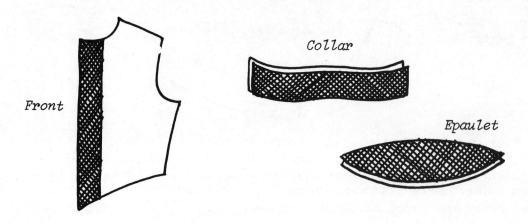

Front

Collar

Epaulet

If you want a doublet that has vertical slashes in the front pieces, do the slashes before putting the doublet together. If you are doing any other unusual decoration, such as strips of trim or ribbon sewn on the front and back, do them now, while the pieces are still flat. Edge trim can be applied later.

Sew together the doublet front and back pieces at the sides and shoulders. Check for fit, then sew on the finished collar, skirting and the epaulets. Sew the front and back pieces of the lining, and pin the center front edges to the fabric ones, with the right sides together. Sew the center fronts together, turn and press. Hand-sew the lining in place at the neck, armholes, and waist, clipping curves before turning in the raw edges. Add buttons and buttonholes or loops down the front, or use the buttons as decoration, letting hooks and eyes do the work. The body of the doublet is now done.

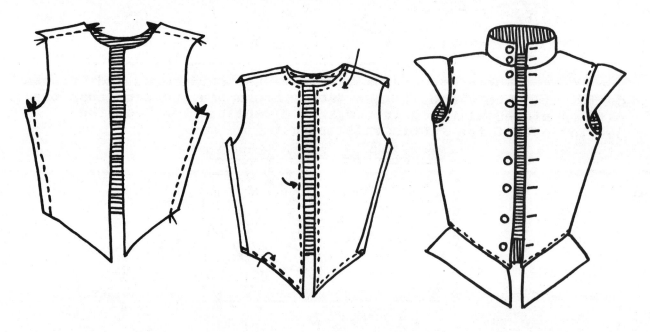

To slash the front, cut the pattern piece as you want it, and add ½" to both cut edges. Then sew them together at least 2" from the top and bottom edges. Fold under the raw edges and decorate them as you want. The lining will be handsewn to these edges later. Thereafter, treat each front piece as one and continue as for the regular doublet. The slashes should have ties, buttons, or hook and eyes to fasten the edges of the slashing together.

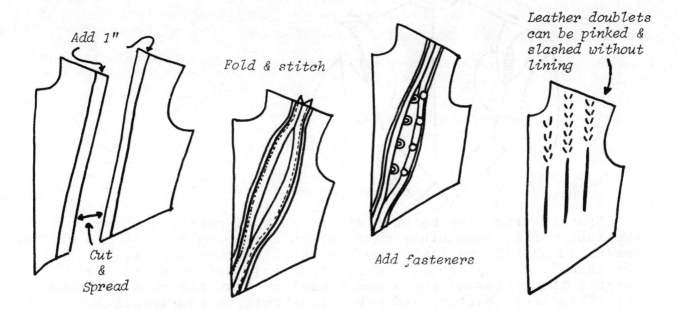

Add 1"

Cut & Spread

Fold & stitch

Add fasteners

Leather doublets can be pinked & slashed without lining

Epaulet & Skirting Variations

Epaulets serve two main functions on a doublet or bodice. They make a person's shoulders look broader, thereby making the waist look smaller. And they also help to conceal where the sleeves are tied into the body of the garment. Any part of the garment which is so close to the face will get a lot of attention, so make it a little eye-catching when decorating it.

Epaulets can be made as one piece, or they can be split in the middle. The points can be sewn all the way down, or the ends can be finished by hand and left hanging out a little. These are all things we have seen in period portraits, so we are reluctant to say "Do this, and this only".

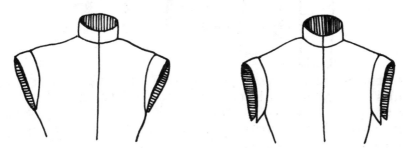

Sewn and loose epaulets

You can cut one curve of the epaulet to give a different look by setting the epaulet in either way. With the shallow curve facing out, the slope is down, with the deeper curve facing out, the slope is straight out or a little up. If you choose the up-tilting style, be very careful with the size and degree of tilt or you will look like lash Gordon. Be subtle.

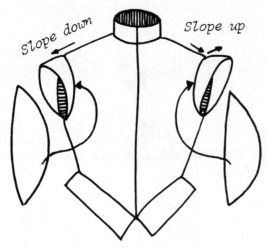

Epaulets can also be cut into tabs as we showed earlier, or the tabs can be made other ways, which some people think are much easier to do. If you wish, you can make the tabs separately, then sew them in one by one. If you do them this way, make the ones nearest the bottom of the armhole smaller than the ones at the top. This looks better, and makes less bulk in the armpit.

Seperate tab epaulette

Another way to do the tabs is to make loops of ribbon or fabric strips, like little slops panes, and treat them the same way you would the separate tabs.

Loop epaulet

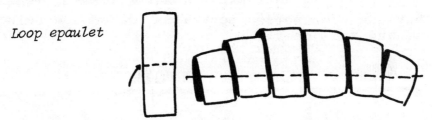

You can use these same treatments for the skirting piece, cutting it into tabs, if you want to, or using one of the other ways of making tabs to give the same effect. If you do one kind of tab on the epaulets, you should do the same on the skirting. It just looks better that way.

If you want padded shoulder rolls instead of epaulets, cut two crescent shapes for each roll, about 18" from point to point.

With the right sides together, sew two of the crescents along the outside edge. Turn, stuff and sew shut by hand or machine, turning the raw edges to the inside. Decorate as desired, and sew by hand to the armhole opening after the doublet is done. If you use this treatment for the armhole, do not repeat it for the skirting. It will look like a little bumroll around your hips, and we have never seen a picture of a man who was wearing one of those.

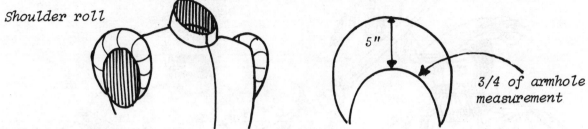

Shoulder roll

5"

3/4 of armhole measurement

Beefeater Doublet

For another look, like that of the respectable merchant, or city official, cut the waist straight across instead of pointed in front, and pleat into the waist of the doublet, a skirting which is 20" wide and twice as long as the waist measurement (or more).

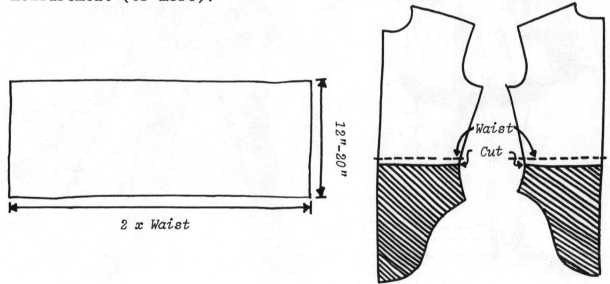

12"-20"

2 x Waist

Waist

Cut

For less bulk at the waist, as with heavy fabrics, you may want to curve the skirting pieces like the illustration, and sew them in as before. Line the skirting before you sew it in.

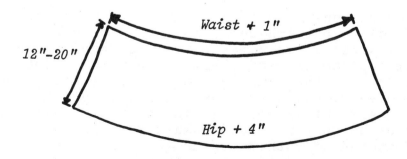

Waist + 1"

12"-20"

Hip + 4"

This is how the Beefeater's doublets looked, and they are about as historically accurate as anything you see today.

Noble's Doublet

The courtier's doublet is tighter, so you can either fuss with the middle class pattern until it fits more closely, or you can try the following. Trace a man's vest pattern of the proper size onto a large piece of paper. Now lay a man's shirt pattern over it, and trace off the armhole, center front line, and neckline. This is because, while the vest fits the body closely, the armhole and neck are cut larger than for a shirt. Using the two patterns together helps you to compensate for this and gives you the best features of both patterns.

52

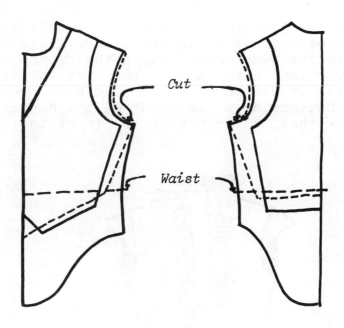

Cut

Waist

Now, as before, measure the man from armpit to waist and mark the pattern you drew. Follow the previous instructions for finishing the pattern and making the doublet, excepting that the body pieces should also be interfaced, so that they will hold their shape better, and you should omit the long-skirted variation. That was a middle class fashion.

For a man who wants and/or needs additional slimming, or has difficulty with the rather rigid posture demanded by upper class clothing, a corset can be built into the lining of a back-opening doublet. It has approximately the same shape as a woman's corset of this period. Make it out of sturdy lining fabric, interfaced with a medium to heavy weight interfacing. Sew it to the lining before the lining is attached to the exterior fabric, and make casings for the boning, as shown. Then follow the instructions for making the doublet. After the doublet is done, hand stitch the bones into the casings, and lace him up into his new posture.

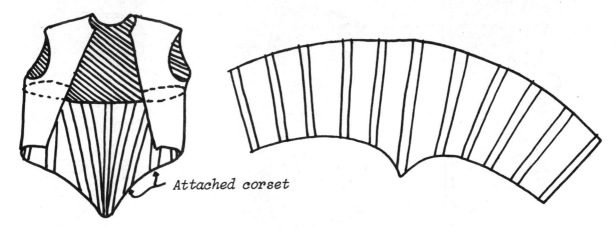

Attached corset

The doublet may be fastened up the front or the back, as you prefer. Some things to remember when making a back opening doublet are, firstly, the back edges should be well stiffened and preferably boned, so that the edges won't crumple when the lacing is tightened. Secondly, sew a placket, a rectangle 4" wide and as long as the entire back edge, behind the grommets, to hide the shirt, because the lacing allows the back to gape slightly. Thirdly, the front should be boned, so the point won't flap up. And lastly, sew buttons down the front of the doublet, so that people will think that it fastens up the front instead of the back.

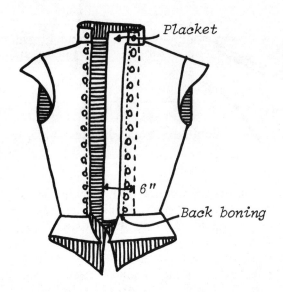

If you want a heavily decorated doublet, do as much as you can before you sew the pieces together. It will be much easier to deal with them while they are still flat and separate.

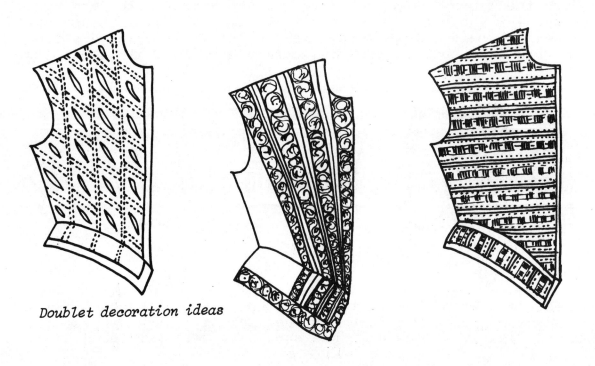

Doublet decoration ideas

For an even more authentic look, use a suit coat or vest pattern with curved side-back seams. Many Elizabethan doublets had seams like these. Allow extra time for fitting, as the curves should lie flat against the back, and when you add this to an already snug garment, you add more difficulty. The finished effect if well worth it, however.

Peascod Doublet

Some of the more fashionable men, as the reign went on, sported a peascod-bellied doublet. It resembled the shape of a peapod, or maybe a cuirass from a suit of armor, and had to be padded and boned to help keep the shape. Some courtiers had to be laced into their doublets from the back, because of all that boning and padding in the front, although most doublets did fasten up the front with buttons or hooks. A true gentleman had difficulty dressing himself, and if he was high enough to rate a valet, would never even try.

The peascod-bellied doublet should be laced up the back, because it is almost impossible to button up the front, though museums contain some examples of ones that did. This is because the front is so heavily padded and boned. The bottom of the peascod should come to the top of the crotch, or just above.

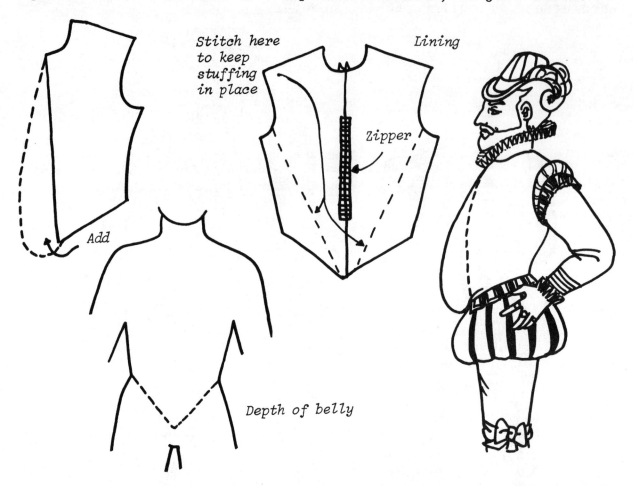

Stitch here to keep stuffing in place

Lining

Zipper

Add

Depth of belly

The front pattern pieces should be altered to look like this. Cut the fabric and interfacing, using the peascod pattern and decorate as desired. The front lining is cut using the regular doublet front pattern, and the front seam should be left open a little, or a zipper put in, so the stuffing can be put in later, or renewed as it squashes down. Now, sew up the center front seam of the peascod, following the curve around to where it will join the skirting at the waist. Then, sew a piece of boning or stiff wire, bending the ends back first, all the way down the front seam of the doublet. This will help the peascod keep its shape after stuffing.

Put the doublet together as for the regular doublet with back fastenings, and after the lining is inserted, stitch the fabric to the lining in a slanting line from the armpit to the bottom of the center front. This will keep the stuffing from shifting toward the back and will give a nice V-shape to the front of it.

Sleeve variations will follow in another section, as men's and women's sleeves were very much alike.

CAPES, COATS & ROBES

This section will describe overgarments that were worn only by men. These include coats, robes, and short capes, that came down to about wrist or knuckle length.

The upper middle or upper class gentleman had a short cape as part of his everyday wardrobe. It was as gaudy as the rest of his clothing, lined with some rich fabric, such as silk or brocade, and was often trimmed with fur, or maybe completely lined with it.

Similar to the short cape, also worn by the nobility, was a coat made like a cape in shape, but with sleeves attached, which were sometimes functional and sometimes not. The coat was worn in the same manner as a cape, and was lined with fur, for warmth. It was heavily decorated and came to mid-thigh.

Short Capes

Short capes can be made in two ways, either a half circle, which is the cheapest and easiest to make, or a 3/4 circle cape, which costs more in fabric and time, but looks and moves much more impressively. Fabric types are the same as those used for doublets. Check yardages in the yardage section.

To make the half circle cape, first, lay your fabric out flat on a large surface, such as the floor. Starting at one end of the fabric, cut a half circle with a radius of 36". Then, cut another half circle with a radius of 6" for the neck opening. Do the same for the lining.

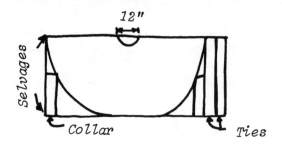

For the 3/4 circle cape, you will need an extra yard each, of fabric and lining. Cut one extra quarter circle, the same radius as the half circle. For the neck opening, the cut should have a 4" radius rather than a 6" radius, so the neck opening won't be too big. Cut two pieces 6" wide by the full width of the fabric for the ties, and two pieces of fabric 5" wide by 20" long to make the collar.

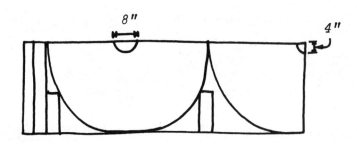

The above instructions are for cutting a cape out of fabric with no nap. If your fabric is the type to have a nap, such as velveteen, corduroy, or brushed denim, you should cut out the pieces as illustrated below, so that the nap on all the pieces will go the same way. For a half circle cape, cut two quarter circles, and for the 3/4 circle cape, cut three. Then sew them together. Make sure when cutting the collar that the nap is going the way you want it to be in the finished product. All other directions are the same for both types of capes.

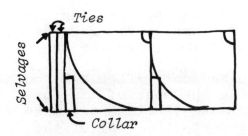

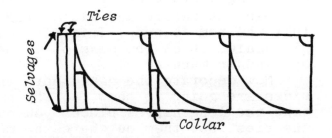

Sew the cape pieces together, if necessary. Do the same with the lining. Interface the collar and front edges of the cape to 4" back from the edge. Sew the collar together, turn right side out and press.

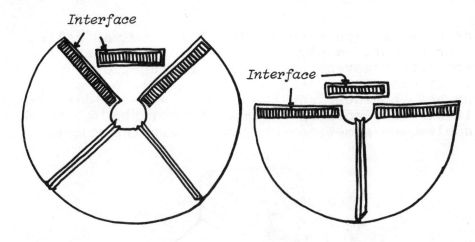

With the right sides together, sew the lining to the fabric along the front edges. Turn and press, the sew the fabric and lining together around the neck opening. Ease the neck opening into the collar, matching center backs, and sew one side of the collar to the cape. Turn in the raw edge of the other part of the collar and handsew it to the lining.

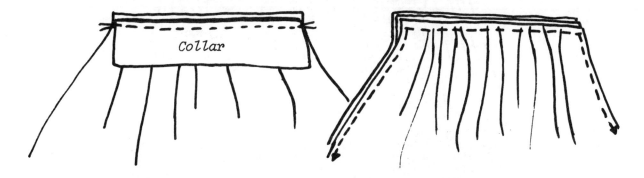

Let the cape hang for a few days, so that it will do any stretching it is going to do before you hem it. Be aware that any fabric will stretch a little. While the cape is hanging,

59

either on a dress dummy, or on the person who will be wearing it, pin the fabric and lining together at the hem, making sure that the hem is even. Trim if necessary, turn in the raw edges, pin again, check the hang of it one last time, then sew the hem, by hand or machine.

Now decorate the cape, both inside and out. After all, both sides are going to show, so why not make the most of it. Now, take the long narrow pieces you cut to make the ties and make the ties. Sew them on where the collar meets the body of the cape. Or you can use a 1"-2" wide strong ribbon for the ties, if you prefer.

The cape is worn either over one shoulder, which is the Italian manner, or tied in the back with the cape over both shoulders which is the English manner.

Surcote

Another type of cape worn during this time was called the cape-coat, or surcote, a style from Germany. It was a loose fitting cape with sleeves, which could be functional or non-functional. It was worn over a doublet just like a cape, usually thrown over one shoulder, and the sleeves were seldom used as sleeves. It was only worn in England by noblemen, although in Germany, noblewomen sometimes shared it with their men.

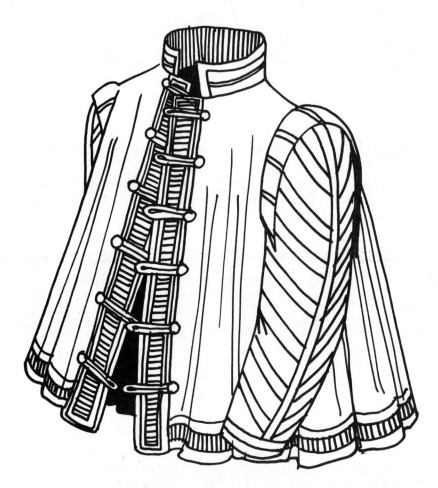

The pattern pieces follow. Note that it is a full circle cape with sleeves and collar attached. We suggest that you make a mock-up of this garment to check placement and fit of the armholes. To hang like their historical models, the sleeve must be a two piece sleeve. The easiest way to get this kind of sleeve is to take the sleeve from a suit coat pattern of the correct size, and spread the upper sleeve cap a little. The armhole curve from the body pieces can then be used to make the right kind of armhole shape on the body of the coat.

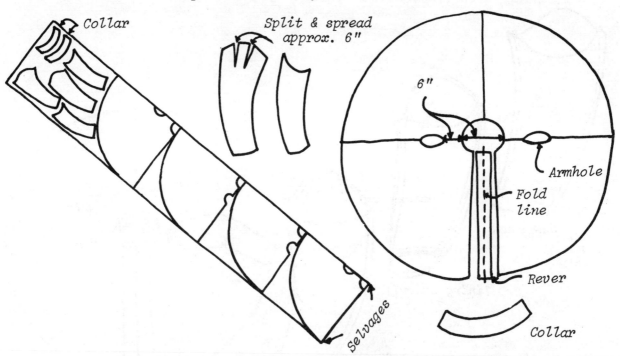

If you don't have a suit coat pattern, you can design a two piece sleeve by using a straight sleeve. This is not easy to do and will need to be fussed with more. Also, you won't have the armhole to draft from. Anytime you save money, it seems you have to pay in time.

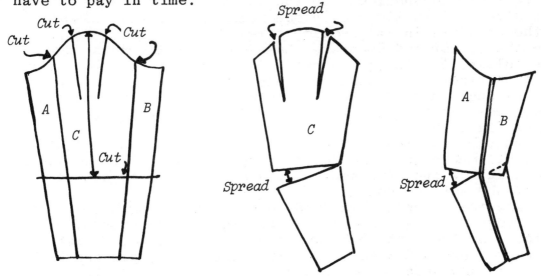

61

The cape-coat is made in a similar manner as the regular capes. Join the body pieces together, as well as the linings.

Decorate the sleeve pieces while they are still flat, then sew the undersleeve to the oversleeve. Do the same for the lining pieces. Sew the sleeve to the lining at the cuff opening, turn and press. Stay stitch the top of the sleeve with both fabric and lining together. That makes the sleeve one piece.

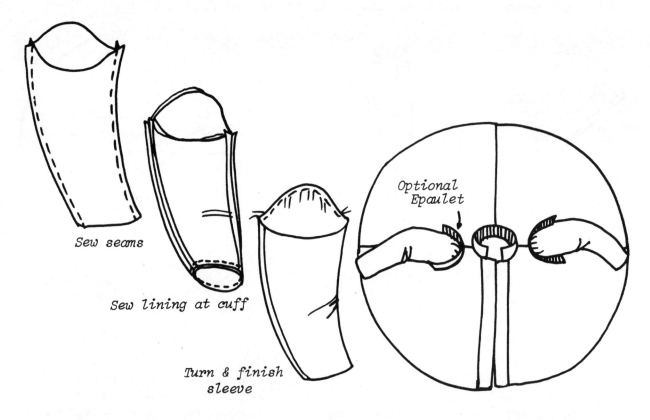

Sew seams

Sew lining at cuff

Turn & finish
sleeve

Optional
Epaulet

Make, decorate, and baste epaulets into the armhole, matching the tops of the shoulders to the center of the epaulets. Ease the sleeves into the body piece and sew in place, also sewing the epaulets in at the same time.

Make the collar and decorate. Ease or pleat the neck edge into the collar, leaving ½" on each side free for attaching the revers. With right sides together, pin the lining against the body at the neck edge. Sew the neck edge only, clip the curve, turn and press. Stay stitch the front edges by sewing the fabric and lining together.

Slip stitch the lining armhole to the fabric armhole, turning under all raw edges, and making sure that there are no lumps or puckers in how the cape hangs. It should be smooth on the inside and the outside both.

Decorate the revers, then fold them in half lengthwise. Then press one edge under ½". Sew the other edge to the edge of the front piece of the coat, making a turn at the top to finish the top edge. Turn and press, flap the rever over, pin and blind stitch the turned under edge in place.

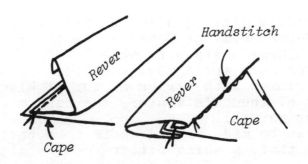

Let the cape-coat hang for a few days, then hem it and wear over one shoulder, over both shoulders, or as a coat, with your arms through the sleeves. To fasten, the cape-coat usually had buttons and buttonloops, with the revers overlapping.

Schaubes

Respectable middle class gentlemen often wore open coats, called by their German name of Schaube, or their Spanish name of Ropon or Ropa. These coats were made like modern choir robes except that sleeves were split down the front, and the revers and collar were trimmed with strips of fur or black velvet, or made entirely out of them. In winter, the coat might be entirely lined with fur for warmth.

The schaube can be made from a choir robe pattern if you have one. Failing that, a shirt pattern can be altered to make the schaube.

We will show two versions. Read both and decide which one fits your needs and abilities better. The first type is easier, and the second type will hang and move better.

Choose a medium to heavy-weight fabric to make the schaube. It will look better in a textured fabric, such as wool or velveteen, rather than a smooth finished fabric. The revers and collar should be a contrasting fabric or fur.

For the first kind of schaube, you should use the directions for making a yoke pattern from the shirt pattern which is in the shirt section. Cut the front edges of the yoke as illustrated.

Pin the front and back yoke pattern pieces together, and draw a curve around, as shown. Trace this collar pattern off onto another piece of paper.

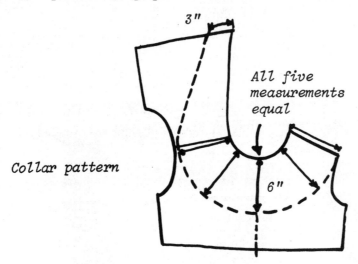

The schaube should be approximately knee-length, or a bit longer. The revers, which attach to the collar, are about 5"-6" wide and the same length as the body front piece. Add length to the shirt body piece.

The sleeve is cut in half lengthwise, and the back half is extended by at least 12". Then, pin the underarm seam together, and the sleeve piece should look like the illustration. The sleeve and yoke should be lined, though the body doesn't have to be. It will, however look and hang much better if you do.

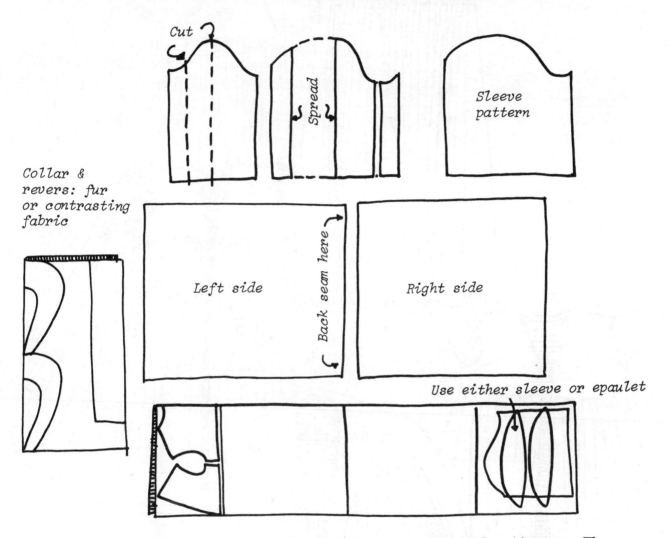

Collar & revers: fur or contrasting fabric

Cut

Spread

Sleeve pattern

Left side

Back seam here

Right side

Use either sleeve or epaulet

Gather or pleat the body pieces into the yoke pieces. Then sew the fronts and back together at the shoulder and side seams. If you choose to put in sleeves, make and insert them according to the instructions for the split sleeve in the section on sleeve variations. Otherwise, put in epaulets. Make sure that the epaulets are larger than the epaulets on the doublet that will be worn with the schaube.

Sew the yoke lining pieces together and stitch them to the yoke along the neck and front edges. Turn under the raw edges of the lining at the armholes, and sew by hand. Sew the top collar piece to two of the revers pieces. Sew the under collar piece to the other two revers pieces. Then, sew the collar and revers combinations together along the outside edges. Clip the curves, turn, press, and sew it to the yoke/body piece along the inner edges, turning in all raw edges as you go.

Let the schaube hand for a few days, then hem to the desired
length. You're done.

Another version of the schaube can be made that uses the
infinite gore method for the skirting. This will hang better as
the man moves about. To decide how many gores you will need,
take the man's chest measurement and double it. This is how
far around the top edge should be before gathering it into the
yoke. Then decide how much larger you will want the hem to be.
It should be at least twice the top measurement, so that it
will flare enough. Keep in mind that the layout shown is only
good for fabric without a nap. Work out the number of gores you
will need, by drawing a scale model layout on a piece of paper.
This will show you what the size and shape should be, and hope-
fully, how much extra fabric you will need for this kind of
skirting.

For the layout, we will consider the selvage edge as half
gores, which will need to be sewn together as shown.

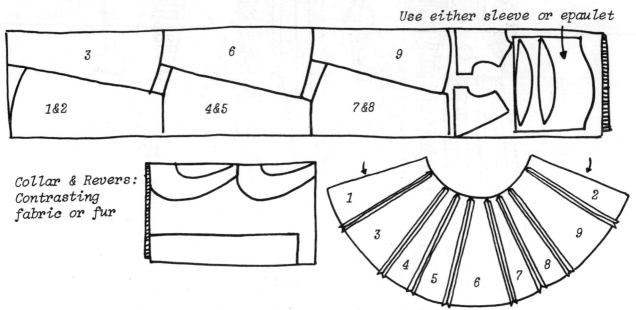

This kind of skirting will hang better if you line the
skirting. Cut and sew the lining panels like the fabric ones.
Pin together with all the seams to the inside, making sure that
the seams match along the top edge, and stitch as shown.

Sew the front pieces of the yoke to the back piece. Do the same for the lining pieces.

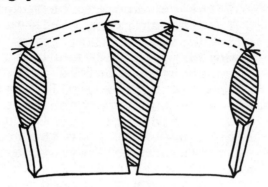

Sandwich the gathered or pleated skirting between the yoke and the yoke lining. Pin and stitch as shown. Fold the yoke up, press, and top stitch, if desired. Put the sleeves and/or epaulets into the yoke.

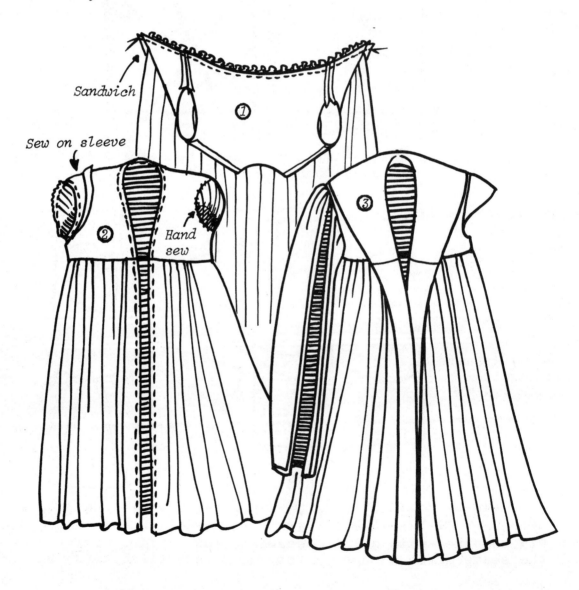

Smooth the lining and the yoke. Pin around the armhole and chest front, and stay stitch. Turn under the lining at the armholes and hand sew it down. Make sure that the lining doesn't pull the yoke. The entire yoke should lie flat. Now, put on the collar and revers as in the other version. Let the schaube hang for a few days, hem and this one is done.

The schaube was also worn ankle-length, and was called a gown. The same class of men wore it, and used it for ceremonial and state occasions. It often had sleeves which were slit at the elbow, to allow the arm to come out of the sleeve at that point, while the rest hung down behind. It was sometimes worn belted closed. This gown was a favorite of scholars and schoolmasters.

Shoulder point

Sew from top
to here

Cut

Sew from bottom
to here

Line completely

MILITARY INFLUENCE ON FASHION

It is not within the scope of this book to provide a complete treatment of the subject of weapons and armor in Elizabethan England. However, no discussion of this period of costuming can be considered complete without at least touching on the use of arms and armor as accessories to civilian dress.

Gorget

Peascod
cuirass

Wheelock pistol

During this period, England had no national standing army. Most noblemen had groups of paid retainers who were subject to their orders and wore their livery. The retainers could be used either for or against the Crown, depending on the politics of the lord involved.

The next closest thing that England had to a regular army, was the number of men that every lord was expected to provide for military service in time of need. This was in addition to his group of personal retainers. These men for the army were taken from the peasantry and middle classes, sometimes unwillingly, handed a pike or other pole-arm, and told which way to point it. This was the extent of military training for the majority of the army.

Archers, though falling into disuse with the rise of more reliable guns of various types, were still considered a useful part of the military system. This was because many country people still hunted with the longbow or crossbow to feed their families. They could shoot well and had their own equipment, a fact the parsimonious Elizabeth could not overlook when counting the costs.

Soldiers in the army were usually paid, but irregularly at best, and sometimes not at all. If they were sent to a foreign land to fight, they were encouraged to live off the land, and any plunder they managed to acquire was considered a bonus to their infrequent wages. The battlefield was the origin to the earlier *Landsknecht* look in fashion. By helping themselves to many yards of brightly colored stolen silk, they had helped to set a style for gentlemen all over Europe, especially in Germany and the Low Countries. Cuttes and slashes simulated cuts recieved in battle, and the different colors peeping through the holes simulated the silken plunder.

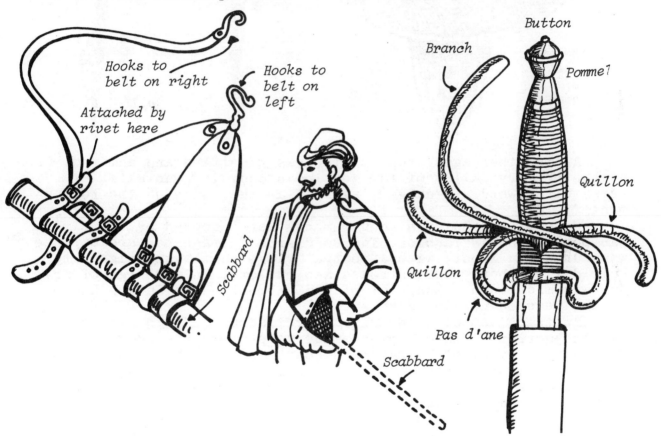

Uniforms for soldiers were mostly non-existant. A lord would dress his servants and retainers in his personal colors, called livery, but there were only a very few groups of professional soldiers in England that had regular uniforms. The Yeomen of the Guard with their red and gold doublets are one example that can be seen even today. The Queen's personal bodyguard, called the Gentlemen Pensioners, wore her livery of green and white, and on formal occasions, donned a long red cloak over all.

71

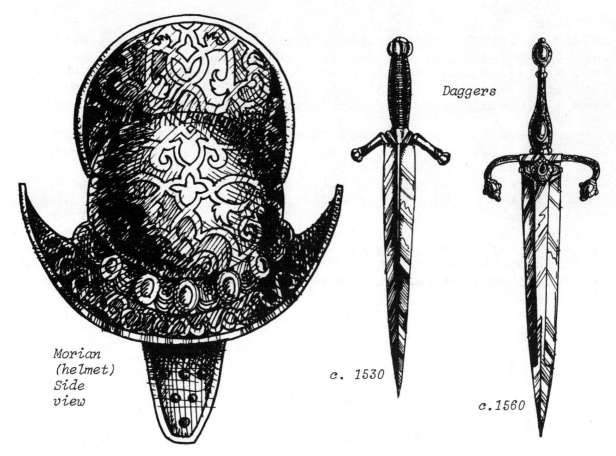

Morian
(helmet)
Side
view

Daggers

c. 1530

c.1560

As in other ages, the soldier was glorified and admired. One of the primary skills of the gentleman courtier was skill of arms, with sword and dagger, as well as the lance on the tournament field.

Some of a soldier's accutrements were adopted by the civilian population as fashion. The soldier's cuirass, or breastplate, was curved in front, with a central ridge that was designed to help deflect both sword strokes and bullets. This design of armor was made into a shape of padded garment which became known as the peascod-bellied doublet.

Another item of soldierly apparel adopted by gentlemen was the gorget, a throat piece made to protect the neck and upper chest. Many of Elizabeth's courtiers had their portraits painted while wearing a gorget or cuirass over the rest of their finery, because it was thought to help make a man look more dashing and brave.

The wearing of swords and daggers also helped to contribute to this effect. If a gentleman did not own at least 100 acres of land, he was forbidden by law to wear a sword, although everybody had an eating knife. Women, of course, were forbidden to wear swords, under any circumstance, no matter how much land they owned or controlled. The closest thing to a weapon that a woman could have was her eating knife. However, there are cases of women who replaced the wooden or ivory busk in their corsets with one made of metal, which could be used as a dagger in extreme circumstances.

72

A few gentlemen owned and carried firearms, but their size, weight and unreliable characteristics made them less desirable than a sword for personal defense.

Since the sword was hung on the left hip (to be drawn by the right hand), it was considered safer, and therefore more proper for a lady to walk at a gentleman's right side, rather than the left. That way, she could be better protected, and would not impede the draw of the blade. Even now, a lady walks on a man's right as a matter of etiquette, not realizing the reason for the tradition.

Full plate armor & Landsknecht

SECTION III: WOMEN'S CLOTHING

WOMEN'S FASHIONS: AN OVERVIEW

I. Lower Class

A peasant woman wore a long-sleeved shift under everything, and at least two skirts over that, with the upper skirt, usually newer than the underskirt, tucked up out of the dirt.

Women wore at least two skirts at all times for several reasons. The primary reason was that two or more skirts was a more efficent insulator than one. You must remember that there was no central heating in a peasant's hovel, and much of their time was spent out-of-doors anyway.

She had an apron on over the skirts to keep them clean if she was doing some work, which was most of the time. She wore a tight-fitting, scoop or square necked bodice or vest, which usually came to a point in front, and laced or buttoned on over the shift. It had removable sleeves which were worn or not, depending on the weather.

Peasant women

Peasant mix-and-match

    Any woman over the age of thirteen had her hair covered by
some sort of headgear, such as a biggins or muffin cap, and the
hair itself was usually braided or bundled up out of the way.
Women sometimes, but not always, wore knee-length cloth hosen
held up by garter ties and she had some kind of shoes if she
was lucky.

75

She had a belt pouch and a small eating knife of her own. She had a basket to carry things gathered in the fields or bought at morning market. In cold weather, she would have a cape or shawl wrapped around her. She had no lace! It was much too expensive.

II. Lower Middle Class

This woman owned more than one shift and the fabric of them was much less coarse than the one worn by the peasant. Her bodice and skirts fit better and could be made of matching fabric. Her sleeves might match, as well. One of her skirts might be decorated or made from a richer material than the other skirt. She wore the richer or newer skirt over the underskirt so it could be shown off to advantage, and tucked it up out of the muck of the streets when she went out.

She could have a modest bumroll under her skirts, and her bodice might be boned on the seams or have a busk down the front of it to have the effect of a corset. Her hair was neater but still worn up off the neck. More care was lavished on the hat or headress, which could be any of several designs.

Middle class women

76

The hat and pouch or other accessories might be embroidered
as well as perhaps matching the fabric of the rest of her garments. She would have some leisure time for that sort of thing.
She often carried a bunch of keys at her belt for the various
chests and cupboards in her house and she might have a maid-
servant to help with her housework. Or she might be a servant
to a higher class lady, herself.

Her hosen and shoes would be nicer than those of the peasant
woman, but they would still be simple and unadorned. She might
have a plain ruff to her shift if it were high-necked. She wore
a cape or shawl, perhaps fur-trimmed, to keep her warm in cold
weather.

III. Upper Middle Class

Ladies of this class were wives or daughters of knights,
country squires, or wealthy merchants or artisans, with their
own servants. Or they might be highranking servants in a noble
household with a lot of authority and power of their own. Wives
and daughters were under the control of their male relatives,
having few rights. But widows at this time had a great deal of
freedom, being allowed to continue their dead husband's busi-
nesses and administrating his properties in their own right.
Like their male equivalents, they dressed as well as they could
afford.

The upper middle class lady's chemise was almost always high-
necked, and made out of some delicate fabric, such as fine linen,
imported cotton lawn, or even silk. It might be embroidered and
had neck and wrist ruffs, which were lace edged, budget per-
mitting. A married lady or conservative spinster wore her chemise closed down the front and a single lady wore hers open. In
the coldest weather, everybody probably closed their chemises
just to keep out the cold.

Over the chemise, she wore a busk or corset, bum-roll, farthingale (hoop-skirt), and petticoats, just like the noble ladies
but in a less exaggerated style. Her corset was less tight, maybe, her bum-roll was smaller, and her farthingale was less wide
around the hem.

Her underskirt, richly decorated, was cut to fit closely over
the farthingale, so the effect was that of a stiff A-line long
skirt. The bodice was tight-fitting, square-necked and pointed at
the bottom of the front, or it was high-necked, with a tall collar. The overskirt was full and pleated or gathered into the
waistband. The bodice and overskirt matched and the overskirt
might be split up the front to display the fancy underskirt. Her

laced-in sleeves sometimes matched the relatively plain fabric of the skirt and bodice, and sometimes they matched the more ornate underskirt. She sometimes wore the open Spanish Surcote as an extra warm layer of clothing over her gown, or she wore it closed, as a housedress or maternity gown over the shift alone.

Her hair was dressed to imitate the styles of the Court ladies and she wore a variety of wigs, hats and headdresses, just like they did. She might have knitted hosen with pretty ribbon garters and her shoes would have low heels, or be more like dancing slippers. Out of doors, she wore chopines, similar to wooden clogs, over her slippers to keep the mud of the streets off of them.

She had embroidery or other trim decorating the garment edges, and they might also be beaded or jeweled if she was rich enough. Her hat or cap, pouch and shoes could also be decorated like the rest. She still wore the household keys at her belt, but probably not a knife anymore. She would eat with a table knife and fork,

Noblewomen

78

instead. Depending on her pretensions, she might also have a fine
feather fan or pomander. She wore whatever jewelry she could
afford and the sumptuary laws would allow. Jewelry would include
gold and silver chains, strings of glass beads, semi-precious
stones, or small pearls. She may have worn rings, brooches, earrings and pins, as well.

IV. Upper Class & Nobility

The upper class lady was a person of rank and distinction.
She was often the administrator of vast estates when her lord was
gone, or she did so in her own right. She was well educated and
her opinions were respected. Elizabeth herself understood, wrote,
and spoke something like seven languages fluently. She ruled an
empire and left England stronger than she found it. Her ladies
of the Court were a power to be reckoned with as they were
clever, witty, and politically aware, as well as being beautifully dressed. They were fully a match for the men they lived
with.

When a great lady arose in the morning, she removed her
night or bedgown and night-cap, and was helped by her servant
into her partlet or shift. Night gowns, specifically for sleep-
ing in, had been introduced into the Court of England from
France by Anne Boleyn. The lady's chemise was made of the very
finest linen, cotton, or silk, and was often so delicately woven
as to seem like gauze. They were sometimes embroidered or sewn
with pearls. Like the middle classes, married ladies closed
their chemises, and single ladies opened theirs.

After the chemise was put on, the next things to be put on
were the petticoat, farthingale, bum-roll, and more petticoats.
The tightly laced corset took care of any unsightly bumps and
bulges, and pushed up the breasts for all to see. Then went on
the elaborately decorated underskirt, overskirt, bodice and
sleeves. Many ladies wore the Spanish Surcote over all this,
especially in cold weather, or they wore the closed surcote by
itself over the shift as a casual at-home or maternity gown.

Her hosen were hand-knitted of silk or worsted and were very
costly. She wore soft leather shoes with 1"-2" heels, or low
heeled slippers made of velvet, satin, or fine Spanish Cordovan
leather. The would be further embellished with shoe roses or
jeweled buckles. She wore chopines over slippers if she went out
walking in the muddy streets.

Her face was heavily made up with the rather primitive and
decidedly dangerous cosmetics of the time. The look was for pale
skin, pink cheeks, red lips, and large, dark, expressive eyes.
White lead was the main ingredient in the foundation, and it
pitted the skin, causing more than one lady's early death.
Fulminate of mercury was used to peel off the skin pitted by the
lead and give a lady a smooth complexion again. Ladies put drops
of belladonna in their eyes to make them look bigger. Red hair
was always "in" during Elizabeth's reign, but the substances used
to dye the hair sometimes caused it to fall out, hence, the popu-
larity of wigs. The Queen herself often wore wigs, especially as
she got older, and upper class ladies strove to imitate her. Hair
and wigs were dressed in a variety of styles from short and curly

to long and straight, brushed over pads to a bun in the back, like the 1940's pompadour style.

Hats were many different styles, too. The most popular styles were the flat cap, French Hood, Attifet, and the tall crowned hat that was so popular with the middle classes. Court ladies would sometimes wear a long, pearl-edged gauzy veil over a diadem. For hunting, they bundled up their hair into a net and securely pinned on a flat cap or other hunting hat over that.

Ruffs were every size from tiny ruffles at neck and wrist to 6" wide constructions which owed their size and stability to liberal applications of starch. The largest ruffs had to be held up by a wire support and special long spoons were designed to help the most fashionable to eat their food. This era saw the rise of an entire profession dedicated to keeping these ruffs beautiful.

From her girdle (belt), she would have hanging a pomander, fan, maybe a small purse, hand mirror, handkerchief, or scissors and needle-case combination. Fans were made of feathers or cloth and were shaped like a flat circle or oval on a stick. Folding fans, imported from the Orient, made their first appearance toward the end of this period, so a very few Court ladies might have them, but no one in the lower classes would. They had fans woven of straw most often. Pomanders were pierced metal balls with scent inside, or a dried orange or lemon studded with cloves and placed in an embroidered or jeweled velvet covering. They were used to keep away "bad airs" which they thought carried diseases. In a time when people seldom bathed and streets were an open sewer, they might not have been far wrong.

The lady would wear scented gloves made of fine, soft leather and slit over the tops of her fingers to display her rings. When she went outside on a rare, sunny day, she wore a mask over her face to avoid sunburn. This also served to guarantee her anonimity if she so desired.

Jewelry was abundant, including gold chains, bracelets, necklaces, brooches, rings, strands of pearls, earrings, jeweled buttons, girdles and tips for her points. After she was dressed, it was a wonder that she could move at all.

It must be remembered that a great lady did not work with her hands more strenuous than needlework, or mixing simples. Also recall that ordinary day wear, even for a noble lady, was much less ornate and confining, than her finest gown for Court wear.

Lace patterns

80

SHIFTS, CHEMISES & PARTLETS

A shift or chemise was a woman's basic garment, no matter what class she belonged to. It was the first thing she put on in the morning, and the last thing she took off at night, assuming that she took it off at all. Lower class women had the habit of keeping their shifts on day and night, for the sake of warmth and convenience. The upper classes, with their warmer rooms, often slept in their skins, or in a kind of night-gown, called a "bed-gown".

A shift could be designed with a low or high neckline, be made of coarse linen or fine silk, be plain or embroidered, collarless, or made with a collar that had a built-in ruff. The low necked shift was worn by lower class and lower middle class women only, and could usually be pulled higher on the neck by tightening the drawstring (if it was designed with one). The high necked shift (also called at this time, a chemise) with or without a collar and cuffs, would have been worn by men of any class, as well as the women described. This section will show you how to make both types.

Shifts in three lengths

81

For comfort's sake, we suggest that you make your shift out of 100% cotton or other natural fiber that breathes. Polyester and poly-blend fabrics look wonderful and are easy to care for, but if your body is in the habit of sweating when you are hot, as most people's bodies are, you will be much more comfortable with a natural fabric next to your skin.

The easiest way to make a peasant type shift is to find a commercial pattern that will give you a blouse that looks like a picture of the peasant blouse in the pattern section, and follow the pattern instructions. This sometimes comes in a long and short sleeved version. Use the long sleeved type only. The shift can be anywhere in length from hip to floor length. If you have no pattern, you can use the following instructions to make a shift from scratch.

If you are using a 100% cotton fabric, such as cotton muslin, remember to wash it in hot water before you cut into it, because it will shrink a little, the first time it is washed.

First, take the following measurements. Measure from the base of your neck to your hip for blouse length, or to the floor for floor length, and add 6" for casing and hem allowance. This body length measurement, we will call measurement #1. Measure from your shoulder to your wrist bone and add at least 10". This extra length will allow for fullness in the sleeve as well as the turnings for the casings. This sleeve length measurement, we will call measurement #2. 19

Now, using measurement #1, cut two pieces of your fabric for the front and back body pieces. Using measurement #2, cut two pieces of the fabric for your sleeve pieces. Do use the entire width of the fabric for the shift pieces, unless you are unusually small. The shift will look and feel better, as well as preventing waste of your fabric.

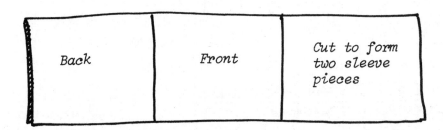

1. Fold each of the body and sleeve pieces in half length, then lay the body pieces, one on top of the other out on a large flat surface, such as the floor. Stack the folded sleeve pieces one on top of the other, and lay them down on the body pieces, overlapping the pieces, as illustrated. There should be a 3" overlap both in and at the top.

Now, on the sleeve piece, draw a diagonal line between the point where the sleeve overlaps the body, and a point 3" in from the edge. This should give you a triangle with two 3" sides. Draw

another line from the first point, down to where the sleeve overlaps the body again. This should be 3" in from the edge, at the
bottom of the sleeve piece.

   2. Cut through all the layers, including the body pieces,
along the lines you drew. You may want to pin it all together
before cutting, so that all eight layers of fabric won't shift
around. The short cut between the 3" marks should just go through
the sleeve pieces. It will help to make the scoop neck. If you
wish, you may now cut a shallow curve in the top edge of the body
piece after unfolding them. This will help to make the scoop neck
as well.

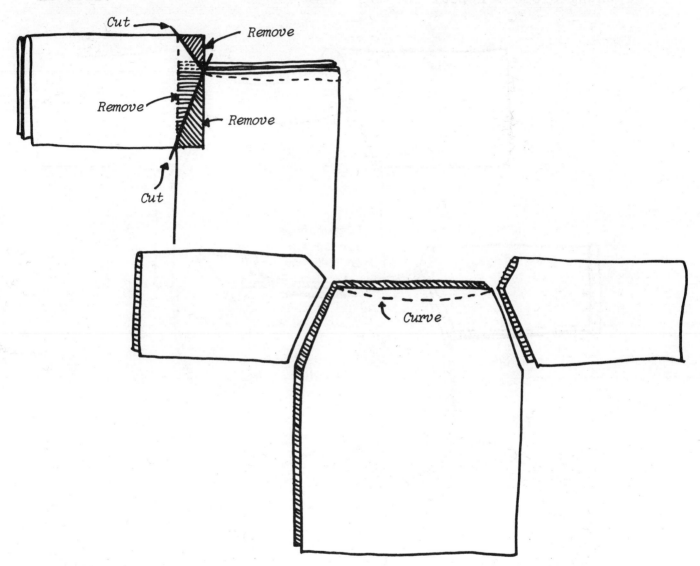

   Opening the body and sleeve pieces out flat, pin them together so that they make the shape of a cross and sew them
together. Then, folding the whole thing in half so that it takes
the shape of a 'T', sew the long seams from the cuff end to the
armpit and down to the hem. Do the same for the other side.

   Work two buttonholes on either side of the center front from
1½" down from the edge to 2" down and clip them open. These are

for the drawstring later, and should show on the outside when the shift is finished.

Turn under all the raw edges (cuffs, neckline, and hem) $\frac{1}{4}$", and press. Then turn under all the edges 1" more and press. Sew all of the turned under parts, leaving small openings in the stitching at the cuffs to insert elastic. This will not be necessary for the neck or hem.

Using a safety pin, thread $\frac{1}{2}$" elastic through the cuff casing and pull it together until it feels comfortably snug on your wrist. Sew the ends of the elastic together and stitch the small opening closed. Repeat for the other cuff.

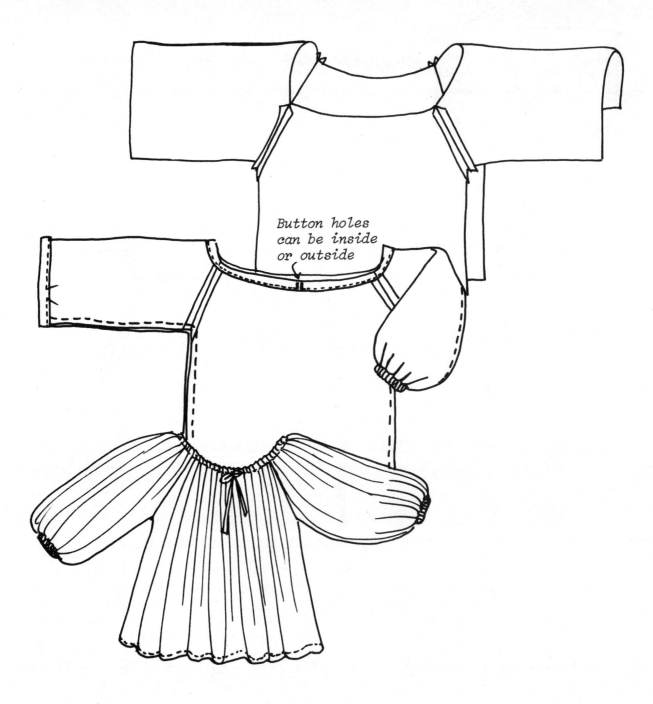

Button holes can be inside or outside

To the purists: yes, we know elastic hadn't been invented yet. But it really works well and is easy to use. We are trying to keep things simple for you at this stage.

Use your safety pin to run the drawstring through the neckline, using the buttonholes you made earlier. Pull the drawstring up, until the neckline is as high or low as you want it to be, and tie a bow. If you want to use elastic here instead of a drawstring, skip the buttonholes and finish the neck edge the same way you did the cuffs. The peasant shift is done.

Alternate Shift

There is a commercial pattern for a high-necked shift, also called a chemise, which is currently available. It doesn't look like a blouse on the pattern envelope, because it is actually a clown suit pattern from the costume section of the pattern book. However, with a few changes, it really makes a great chemise. It should be cut off at the hip for blouse length, it should be open in the front instead of the back, and should have a high collar added, instead of the drawstring neckline it has pictured. These are all simple changes.

Open and closed partlets

85

If you don't want to use the clown-suit type chemise pattern, you can use the do-it-yourself pattern described earlier. To make the chemise, cut the back piece as before. Cut the front piece in a very shallow curve. Cut the sleeves as before, except make a tapering cut from a point 14-16" from the fold at one end, to the selvage edge at the other end. This will give you a wide, full sleeve, without a lot of bulk going into the collar. If you don't want a collar and cuffs, make the chemise the same way as the shift, but pull the drawstring all the way up to the neck when you are done.

If you want a collar and cuffs, cut two pieces of fabric 6" wide by the wrist measurement plus 3" long for the cuffs, and one piece of fabric 4"-5" wide by the neck measurement plus 3" long for the collar, or you may prefer to use the draped collar pattern for the standing collar. The collar and cuffs should be interfaced. Cut a slit 6"-8" down the center front and turn the raw edges under twice and stitch. This will make it possible to pull the finished garment on over your head later. If you prefer, you can leave the chemise open all the way down the front, instead of just having a front opening slit. The chemise as worn under the corset or tight fitting bodice will not gape open. Make an slit in the underside of the sleeve 3/4 of the way towards the back seam of the sleeve for the cuff opening, Turn under the raw edges and stitch.

When constructing the garment, omit the instructions for the neck and wrist casings, as well as the worked buttonholes at the neck. Instead, gather the neck and sleeves into the collar and

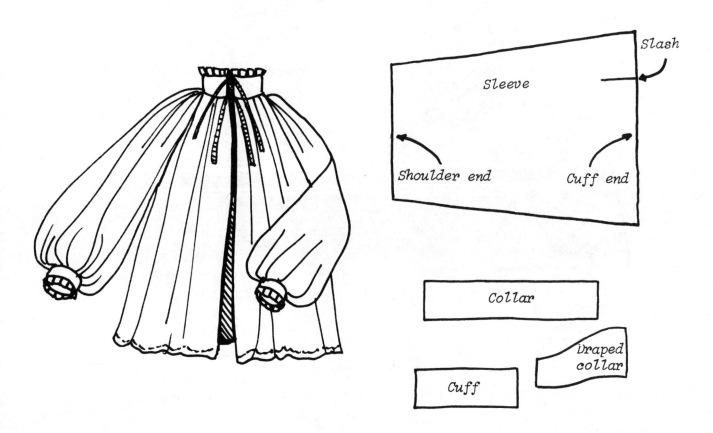

86

cuffs, so that the collar will open at the front of the neck. If simple built-in neck and wrist ruffs are desired, sew one or two rows of box-pleated lace or self fabric to the edges of the collar and cuffs. Finally, use flat hooks and eyes, or ribbon ties to fasten the collar and cuffs closed, and the high-necked shift or chemise is done.

Partlet

Another kind of chemise that was commonly worn by middle and upper class women was like a blouse with a standing collar, long full sleeves, and neck and wrist ruffs sewn on. It was sometimes embroidered with blackwork, or had several vertical bands of trim or embroidery on it, and was called a partlet.

To make this type of partlet, you will need a pattern like the blouse pattern in the general pattern section. Then, you substitute a standing collar for the blouse's flat collar, and sew ruffs at the collar and cuffs. Another thing you should do is to make the sleeves wider by spreading the sleeve pattern. Use

Partlet

strings to tie the front of the neck opening closed. The rest of
the front opening will be held closed, because it will be worn
under the corset or bodice.

Over-partlet

During the reign of Mary I, in the 1550's, women sometimes
had worn a kind of partlet <u>over</u> their gowns, instead of under
them. The garment next to the skin had been called a chemise or
shift at that time. The outer partlet fell out of fashion, except
among the older women during Elizabeth's reign, but the name was
transfered to the high-necked shift worn by all middle and upper
class ladies. The over-partlet was a kind of very short, sleeveless blouse with a high standing collar that was wired all down
the front edge to make it stand out in a graceful curve. It fastened under the arms with self ties, and at the center front with
a brooch or pin which was also used to fasten it to the dress beneath so it would stay in place. It was almost always made of
black velvet with a white lining.

To make this kind of partlet, you need the blouse pattern
refered to earlier. Leave off the sleeves and flat collar, and

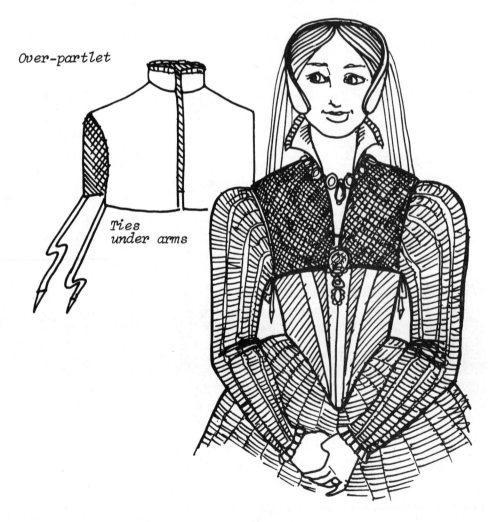

Over-partlet

Ties under arms

cut it off short just under the arms. Add a tall standing collar and line completely in a contrasting color, preferably white. Insert a wire in the front edge of the collar and down the front, so that it will flare and hold its shape. After you finish off the lower edges, add self color ties, so that it can be tied under the arms. When wearing it, pin it together in the front with a decorative pin or brooch.

UNDERPINNINGS

Underpinnings are what gave a lady her fashionable figure. All women wore petticoats for warmth. The lower middle class woman perhaps added a bumroll and a busk in the front of her bodice. The upper middle class and upper class woman went all the way with a corset, bumroll and farthingale, as well as her

Peasant, middle class & noble underpinnings

petticoats. Underpants or bloomers hadn't been invented yet, but if you feel more comfortable with them on, by all means, wear them. We'll never tell.

Petticoat

A petticoat is just another skirt worn underneath everything else. It can be made out of any plain colored fabric, according to the directions for the plain gathered or infinite gore skirt in the section on skirts. You should wear a petticoat under a farthingale so your legs won't show if the skirt tips up, unless you really want people to see your garters, or stockings.

Petticoats as insurance

Bumroll

The bumroll is a padded roll worn around the body just below the waist. It helps to achieve the big hipped silhouette, and incidentally, also helps to support the weight of all those skirts. Some Court lady's skirts, with their beading and jewels can weigh 10-20 pounds and the bumroll takes some of that weight off of the waist and distributes it onto the hips.

The bumroll is made in a crescent shape so it won't stick out over the stomach. To make a bumroll, cut two identical crescent shapes out of any fabric you like. It will never show, so it doesn't matter what you use, but it should be washable, because you will sweat into it, and will want to wash it sometimes. The inner diameter of the bumroll should be a little less than your waist measurement and the outer diameter should be enough bigger so that the widest part at the center back is about 4"-6" wide. If you make the bumroll much bigger than this, it will tend to make your hips look like a shelf. Taller and larger ladies can get away with a slightly larger bumroll.

90

To assemble it, first put the right sides together and sew it along the outer and inner edges, leaving about 6" open on the inner edge. Clip the curves and points, turn, and stuff with fiberfil or foam, pushing it into the points with the blunt end of a pencil. Stuff it firmly, but not too hard, then sew the opening closed. Securely stitch ribbon ties to the points and the bumroll is complete.

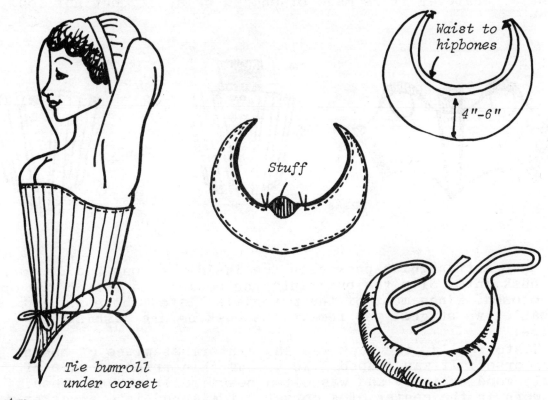

Waist to hipbones

4"-6"

Stuff

Tie bumroll under corset

Corsetry

The corset is Fashion's way of molding the body to fit its ideal image. It is a garment almost unknown before Tudor times, being little more than a breast and belly band to confine and support the torso, mainly the breasts. The Elizabethan corset was still relatively unsophisticated, supporting the breasts by flattening and pushing them up. If laced tightly, it could have been quite uncomfortable for large breasted women. Fortunately, the corset does not need to be very tight to give you the fashionable figure, only very snug.

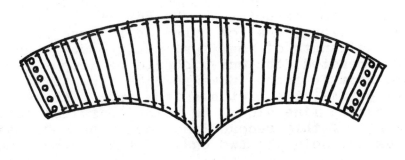

A woman who could not have a whole corset would sometimes content herself with putting a busk down the center of her bodice to stiffen it and make her look more fashionable. This will really only work well for a bodice that laces up the back instead of the front. Cut a triangle about 2"-4" across the top and about 18" long (cut it longer or shorter to fit your bodice). The busk may be made out of boning, hoop wire or metal strapping taped together, or it may be made out of one piece of metal, wood or plastic. Whatever it is made of should be stiff, but not too thick.

Busks

Make a triangular pocket on the inside of your bodice to fit the busk into. Slip the busk into the pocket and stitch the opening closed. Since most of the materials listed above are not washable, we suggest you remove the busk before washing the bodice.

Historically, the busk was the centermost piece of boning in a corset. It was shaped like a long thin triangle made of metal, wood or ivory and was often beautifully carved. When it was worn in the center of a corset, it slipped into a pocket in the front and was held there by a cord or ribbon which passed through two small holes in the busk and in the top edge of the busk pocket. The string was then tied into a bow and held the busk in place in the pocket. The busk-string was sometimes given to a gentleman as an intimate favor. It has since developed into the little bow now found on the front of most brasierres.

Making the easiest corset pattern requires three measurements; the bust, waist and armpit to waist measurements with 1" subtracted from the last one. You will also need to have an idea of how long you want the corset to be from the top edge of the center front down to the point at the bottom.

First, draw a long, shallow curve on a large piece of paper. It should be the length of your bust measurement minus 2". If you are large breasted, the curve should be deeper, as that will give you more room in front. Measure down from this curved line along several points, the distance from armpit to waist minus 1". Draw another curved line along the points parallel to the first line. The length of this second line should be your waist measurement minus 2". Join the two ends of the curved lines.

Now, draw a straight line down the center front to where you want the point to end. Divide the wiast curve in thirds. Draw curved lines joining the wiast curves at the 1/3 marks down to the center front point. This completes the basic corset pattern.

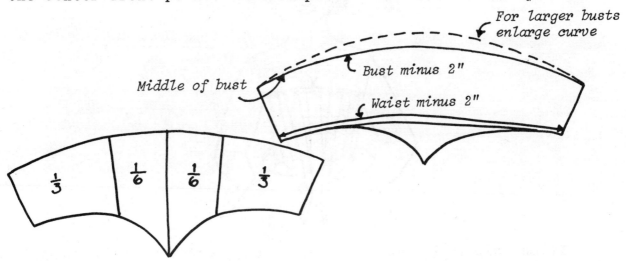

For larger busts enlarge curve

Middle of bust

Bust minus 2"

Waist minus 2"

If your body is <u>not</u> perfect, read this next part. Before you make your corset, you may need to alter the basic pattern to compensate for any figure flaws that might make the corset uncomfortable to wear for long periods of time. So, evaluate your body type first.

Put on a leotard or snug fitting, figure revealing garment, and stand in front of a full length mirror, barefooted, with a friend you can trust to be observant and truthful. Stand as you normally stand. Don't suck in your tummy or throw your shoulders back unnaturally. We are checking for imperfections, remember? The corset can help to compensate for any postural problems later.

The point of this is to gather enough information so that, whether you will be wearing this corset for one hour or eighteen, you will be as comfortable during the last hour as the first. Some large-busted women have found that a well fitting corset can be more comfortable than modern undergarments.

This is what a plain Elizabethan corset looks like. This is the easiest type to make. The variations we will introduce will all be using this type for a base. One thing to remember in these variations, is that the illustrations show exagerated alterations to the basic corset pattern. In reality, you will need to add or subtract much less.

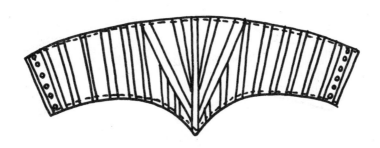

If one hip is higher than the other, make this adjustment in the basic pattern:

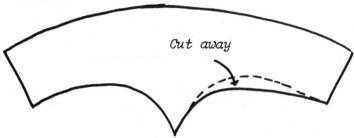

Cut away

If your underarms are fleshy, cut both sides of the basic pattern, like this:

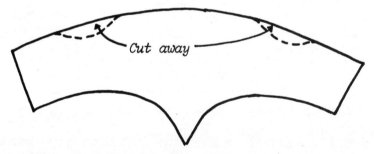

Cut away

If one shoulder is higher than the other, you may want to cut the lower side's underarm part lower, like this:

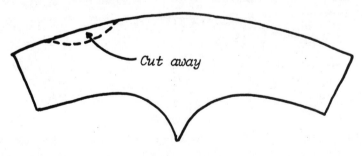

Cut away

If you have a bit of a pot belly before corseting, or if your hips swell out quite a bit just below the waist, you will want to alter the pattern this way:

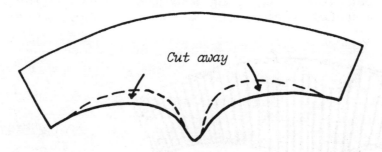

Cut away

If your spine has a curve of any kind, be wary of how much you tighten the lacings of the finished corset. One inch, rather than two or three will be more comfortable for you. If you have a weak lower back, or just want extra support, this is how to change the basic pattern:

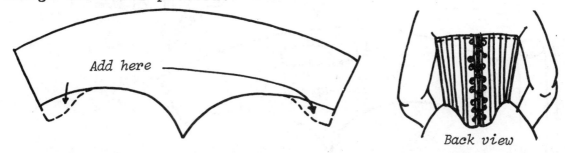

Add here

Back view

If snug waistbands chafe you, you may want to add tabs or picadils at the bottom as shown: more will be said about this later.

When you are working on your first corset, it is a good idea to take the time to make a mock-up out of heavy weight non-woven interfacing. This way, you can check your pattern, before cutting into your fabric and lining. This is also helpful if you are costuming a number of people. You can then use these mock-ups later on. With all the information you have gathered, you are ready to begin!

Using the pattern, cut the corset out of two layers of denim or other heavy fabric with at least one layer of heavyweight interfacing between them. With the right sides together, sew along the back edges. Turn and press.

Sew vertical lines about 3/4" to 1" apart, either slanting slightly as in illustration #1, or sewn with a triangular panel as in illustration #2. Sew ½" binding along the bottom edge from the back edge to the back edge. After that, put a piece of boning, hoop wire, or metal strapping cut to size into every second or third slot, making sure to work it so that the slots at the back edges have boning in them. The boning should be 3/4"-1" shorter than the slots. Now sew binding along the top edge from the back edge to the other back edge. Turn the top and bottom bindings to the inside and hand sew them to the lining.

Put large grommets every 1"-1½" along the empty slots next to the boned ones at the back edges. If your breasts tend to slip down into the corset when you are wearing it, make a sausage shaped pad about 10" long and about 2"-3" wide, and sew it to the lining a few inches below the top edge, after the corset is done.

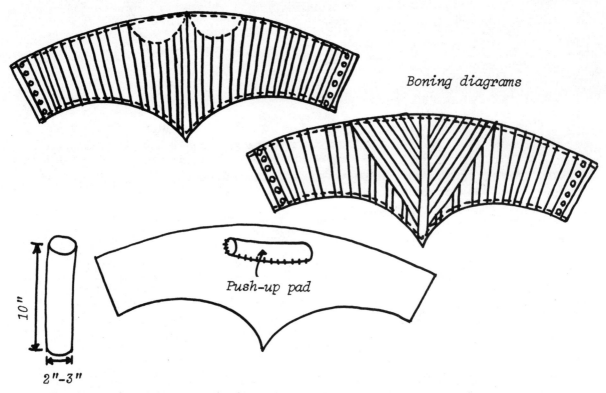

Boning diagrams

Push-up pad

10"

2"-3"

This completes your basic corset. There are two variations which you may wish to try if you are feeling more confident, or want to try them for the extra comfort they will give.

The first variation is to add straps to the corset. Normally a corset will be snug enough so that it won't shift around after it is laced up. But some people feel more secure with straps.

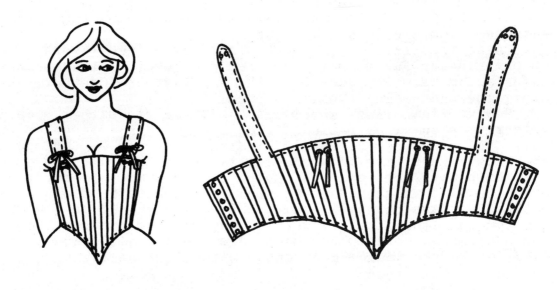

After you have designed your basic corset pattern, make marks along the top edge 4"-6" out from the center front, and 3"-4" in from the back edges. These are the places where the straps will be attached. The straps should be 1"-2" wide and can be designed as part of the corset itself, or be sewn on later. Each strap should be long enough to reach almost from the back where it is attached, over the shoulder to the front where it will be tied.

Taper the strap as it goes toward the front and put one or two grommets in the end of it. Securely sew a lace or ribbon at the mark on the front part of the corset, or put a grommet or two at the mark and thread the ribbon through it as shown.

When wearing the corset, put the ribbon through the hole or holes in the strap and tie, so that it feels snug but doesn't dig into your shoulder. This variation came into common usage during the following two centuries, so if you are a stickler for historical accuracy, leave it off. If you are more concerned with your comfort, use it, by all means.

The second variation will add a lot of comfort, but is more difficult to add to the basic corset than straps. What you do is to add tabs to the bottom edge of the corset and run the boning all the way down into them. This will keep the waist of the corset from digging into your waist, when you lace it tightly. It will also tend to smooth the line over your hips, and give you something to pin or lace the petticoat or underskirt to, so that the weight of it won't drag it below the hem of the overskirt.

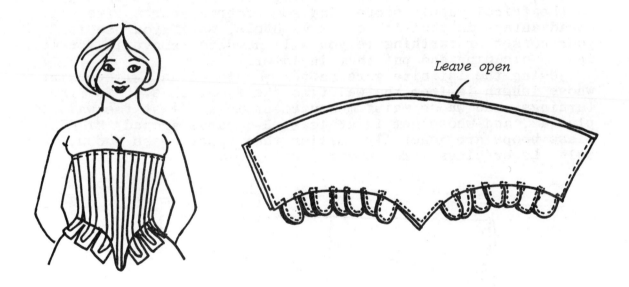

Leave open

You should add the tabs to the bottom edge after you have cut the layers of fabric and lining, but before you sew them together. This means that you will have a fabric corset with tabs, and a lining corset with tabs. Now, putting the right sides together, sew them along the back and bottom edges, around each tab, leaving the top edge open to add the boning later. Turn right side out and press.

Now sew the vertical lines for the casings that hold the bones. Extend the casings right down into the tabs, so that you can insert the boning all the way down into them when you put it into the rest of the corset. Then proceed in the same way as with the basic corset. When you are laced into this type of corset, the tabs will spread out over your hips and distribute the stress more evenly so it will not pinch or bind at the waist. This extra comfort may make the extra work worth it to you.

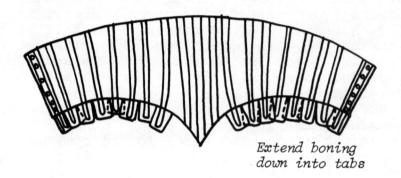

*Extend boning
down into tabs*

Farthingale

The farthingale was a Spanish invention, originally made with hoops of cane or whalebone. Modern hoop wire, which is made out of narrow pieces of spring steel encased in buckram strips, works very well in farthingales. Hoop wire is available in theatrical supply stores and some fabric stores. Its main disadvantage is that it is not washable, so if you use it in your corset or farthingale, you will need to remove it for washing or cleaning and put them in later.

Using the infinite gore pattern, cut out an A-line skirt whose length is from the waist to the floor plus 4" for the turnings, and whose waist measurement is at least the waist plus 4", and whose hem is at least 3-4 yards around. Middle class hoops are generally smaller than upper class hoops, as a rule. Lower class women never wear hoops.

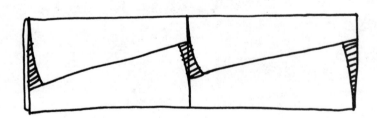

Sew the skirt pieces together, leaving one seam open so that you can work on it while it is flat. Following the curve of the hem, mark the skirt, starting 2" up from the bottom edge, at 6" intervals, so that the finished farthingale will have at least five rows of hoops in them. The more hoops you have, the stronger the farthingale will be, so if you are wearing a heavy set of skirts, put the rows closer together, especially at the bottom, and the farthingale won't collapse on you. Now sew your ribbons or bias tape along the marked lines, turning under the ends of the tape 1½" from the back edges of the skirt. You can sew the tape on the inside so it won't show, or on the outside, if you want a nice decorative accent. Either way is just fine.

Sew up the back seam now, leaving it open down at least 6", or to the level of the first hoop. Turn under the raw edges and stitch. Then turn under the raw edge at the top twice and stitch to make a casing. Turn up the bottom edge to make a hem, such that the finished length will be about 1"-2" above the floor, and pin but do not sew yet. The length will be different after the hoop wire is put in.

Cut the hoop wire with wire cutters to the length of each casing plus 4" for overlap, and tape the ends of each piece with masking, duct, or mystic tape. Insert each piece of hoop wire into the appropriate size casing and adjust the overlap until the finished size of the farthingale looks right to you. Then tape the overlapping ends with the masking, duct or mystic tape so that they will stay that way. Put a ribbon or drawstring through the top casing and the farthingale is finished.

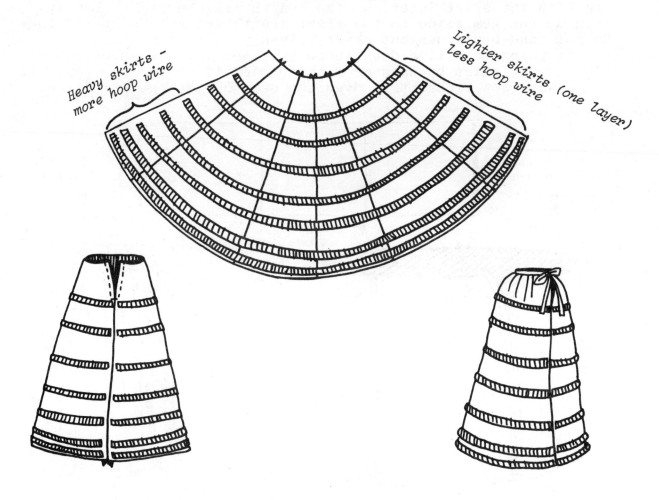

Heavy skirts - more hoop wire

Lighter skirts (one layer) less hoop wire

Skirts of some kind were worn by all classes of women. They were always worn in layers, one on top of the other, for the sake of warmth. They were simple and basic in design, and require no pattern to make. There were two basic types of underskirts and two types of overskirts. You will be shown how to make all four types, as well as a simple apron.

The lower class underskirt and overskirt are exactly the same design. To make this type of skirt, you need at least three lengths of 45" wide, or at least four lengths of 36" wide fabric, 4" longer than the measurement of your waist to the floor, plus 6" more for the waistband. The waistband should be 6" wide and 3" longer than your waist measurement, and you should interface it so it will keep its shape.

Plain Gathered Skirt

Sew the skirt panels together along the selvage edges, leaving one seam open 7"-9" down from the top. Gather or pleat the top edge onto the waistband. Finish the waistband, and sew flat hooks and eyes to it to fasten the skirt. Sew an invisible zipper or hooks and eyes to the skirt opening. Try on the skirt and have a friend help you to mark the hem at floor length or 1"-2" above that. Remember to be wearing the shoes you will be wearing with the skirt later, so the length will be right. Lastly, turn up the hem twice to the right length and stitch by machine. Do not hand hem a peasant skirt unless you are a masochist. No one is going to notice down there at floor level whether you hemmed your skirt by hand or machine. And if it bothers you, you can always sew ribbon trim over the hem to hide the stitching.

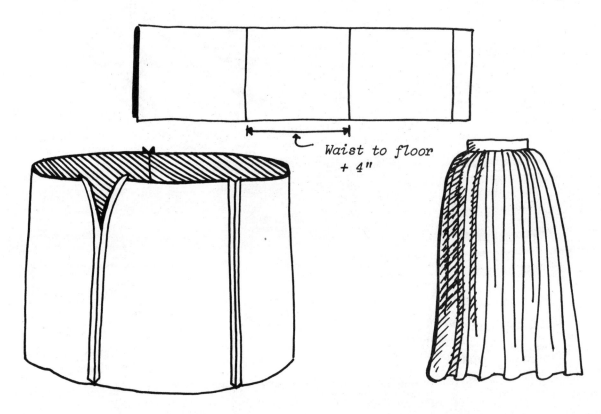

Waist to floor
+ 4"

Infinite Gore Skirt

The infinite gore skirt is a way of making a skirt that is very full at the hem, without a lot of bulk at the waistband. It is cut like the regular skirt, in panels, but the panels are tapered from the waist to the hem as illustrated. If the fabric has no nap, the skirt can be made even more full by reversing the cut off pieces and sewing them between the gores. The rest of the construction details are the same as for the regular type skirt.

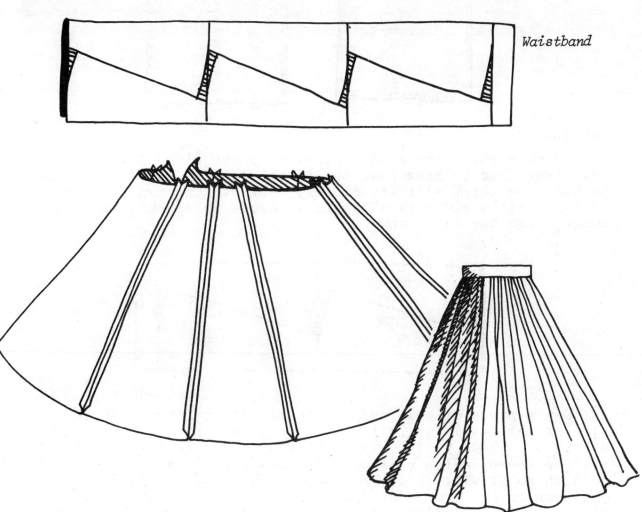

Waistband

The main advantages to this kind of skirt are that it is more slimming for those with wide hips or waists, and it moves better when dancing or walking around.

Aprons

Working women wore aprons over their skirts to keep the dirt off, just like women do today. The aprons were made of simple rectangles of linen (you can use muslin), and were worn without trim or decoration, although they were often dyed some color other than white. Aprons were either pinned to the skirt's waistband, tucked into the top of the skirt, or sewn without gathers to a plain waistband of their own and tied behind.

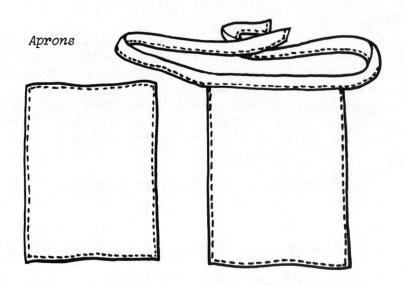

Aprons

Underskirt

To make the upper middle class or upper class underskirt,
you first need to know what the farthingale's measurements are,
because the skirt will fit closely over it. Cut two to four
gores a little wider than the farthingale gores, and about 3"-4"
longer than the farthingale.

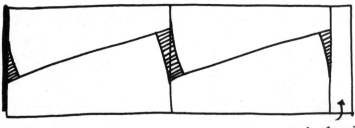

Waistband

Sew a piece of heavyweight interfacing or canvas to the inside of the panel that will be directly under the front of the
overskirt, which will be split to reveal it. This will make it
stiffer there, which will help it to keep its shape and smooth-
ness where it will show. The fancy front panel, called the forepart can be cut from a brocade or other showy fabric, and sewn
to panels of a plainer, cheaper fabric to save money. Decorate
the forepart before the skirt is assembled. It will be easier
to do while it is still one flat piece.

Now, sew the gores together, leaving a back seam open 7"-9"
down from the top edge. Turn under the raw edges and stitch. Sew
the top edge of the skirt to the waistband, pleating or gathering all but the front panel to fit. The front panel must be left
absolutely smooth. Sew flat hooks and eyes to the finished waistband, and fasten the back opening with a zipper or hooks and
eyes, or just leave it open. It isn't going to show, after all.

Now, try on the skirt over the farthingale and have a friend
mark the hem about ½"-1" above floor level. Trim the bottom hem
to 2" below the hem markings, and turn up the hem twice, so that

the hem is the right length and sew by hand or machine. Decorate
the hem at this point, if you want to, and you are done.

Forepart

Overskirt

The upper middle class and upper class skirt opens up the
front instead of the back. This necessitates some changes in
construction details, but uses the same amount of fabric as the
peasant skirts. Measure down from your waist over your farthingale and bumroll to the floor. Add 6" to this. Cut at least
three pieces of 45" wide fabric or four pieces of 36" wide fabric this length. Then cut a waistband piece which is 6" wide and
your waist measurement plus 3".

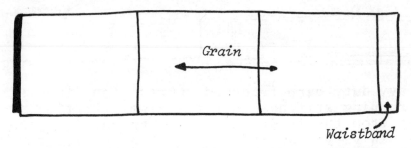

Grain

Waistband

Sew the skirt pieces together along the selvage edges, leaving one seam unsewn. If you are lining the skirt, cut and sew as
for the skirt body. Interface the waistband and the front edges
of the skirt to about 4" from the selvage edges. Pin the skirt
and lining with right sides together along the front edges, and
sew along the selvage. Turn right side out and press. Topstitch
the front edge if desired. Sew the skirt and lining together
along the top and bottom edges, matching all seams, and thereafter treat it as one piece of fabric.

Now, using pins, pleat the skirt fabric into the waistband,
starting at the center back with an inverted box pleat and continuing around on each side until you are about 4" from the
front edges. This last bit must be sewn smoothly, without pleats
or gathers onto the waistband so the skirt will fall open into
an inverted 'V' over the underskirt. Adjust the pleats until
they all please you, then sew securely and finish the waistband.

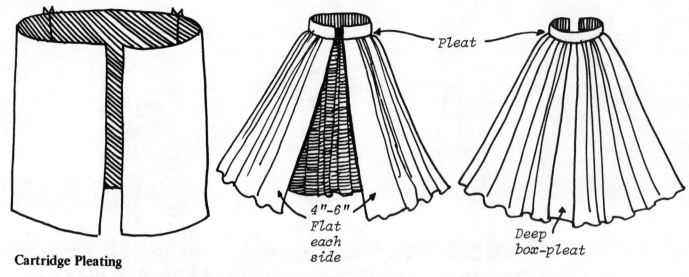

Pleat

4"-6"
Flat
each
side

Deep
box-pleat

Cartridge Pleating

Another method of making the upper class overskirt is to cartridge pleat it to the waistband. Cartridge pleating is a traditional way of attaching large amounts of fabric to smaller pieces, such as waistbands and armholes. It will eliminate the bulk that will drive you crazy trying to push through the sewing machine's presser foot. The finished look will be better and the fabric will fall into lush folds.

Cartridge pleating must be done by hand, but it is very simple once you have been shown how to do it. Prepare the skirt up to the pleating directions. Sew the waistband together as shown. Turn down the top edge of the skirt body 1"-1½" and pin.

Using heavy duty carpet thread, waxed type if possible, take equal sized running stitches in three rows, starting from a point 4" away from the front edge, pulling out the pins as you go. Stitches can vary from ¼" wide to 1" wide with the best being between ½"-1". A good rule of thumb is to evaluate how heavy the fabric is. The heavier fabrics will take a longer stitch. Also, if you are making a skirt with more widths of fabric than we have suggested, the stitches will need to be larger.

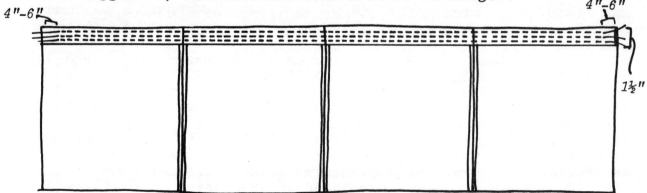

4"-6"

4"-6"

1½"

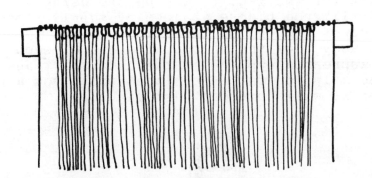
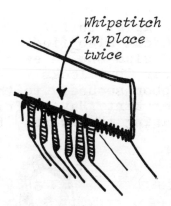

Whipstitch in place twice

The next step is to pull the stitches closely together, to match the waistband. Whip stitch the body of the skirt to the waistband as shown, using that same heavy duty thread. For extra strength, stitch again by hand, going in the opposite direction this time. Now hope that you never have to change the size of the waistband, because you would have to do it all over again, the same way.

Finished, it should look like this:

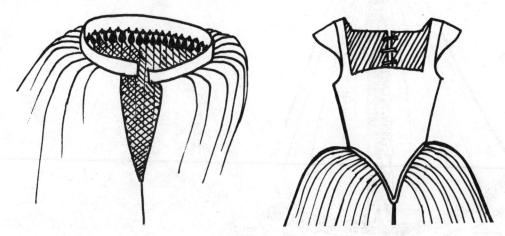

For either skirt, fasten the waistband with flat hooks and eyes, or put three grommets in each side of the front of the waistband and close with a tie. Try on the skirt over your farthingale, bumroll and underskirt. Have a friend mark the skirt at floor level (remember to wear the right shoes), then trim the skirt and lining 2" below the markings. Turn up the hem twice and sew by hand or machine. Trim or decorate as befits your character's station in life and the skirt is finished.

When you begin wearing your underskirts and overskirts, you may find that the overskirt tends to close in front, or worse, open too wide, showing the world the less attractive parts of your underskirt. There are several ways to make sure that the skirt will stay open to the right degree. Elizabethan ladies solved this problem by attaching points to both the underskirt and overskirt. Points are woven strips (ribbon is fine), about 12" long, with metal tips called aglets. Aglets can be bought at theatrical supply or craft supply stores. Some places call them bolo tie ends. Put glue into it, insert the ribbon, crimp the aglet to fit and wait for the glue to dry before using it. You can also find metal filigree pieces at jewelry supply stores and glue one on each side of the end of each ribbon. This is not cheap, but looks very classy. Sew the undecorated end of each ribbon securely to the appropriate place on the underskirt and overskirt. Have a friend help you mark the places while you are wearing the skirts, then it will come out just right.

Skirts fastened together this way love to come untied, but noblewomen don't care. They have maids to retie them again and again, as often as necessary, don't they?

You can imitate the tied together look by using sewn bows with aglets, which conceal velcro strips, hooks or heavy duty snaps. The velcro, hooks or snaps can be used alone, hidden by the edge of the skirt, and it will appear to be perfect as if by magic.

If you are on a budget, you may find that making and jeweling an underskirt may be too much for you. Worry not. Many of Elizabeth's ladies wore their overskirts closed for a different look. Make your overskirt so that it can be worn closed. Then, as time and money permit, make your fancy underskirt and reveal it to the admiration of your friends.

BODICES

All classes of women wore some kind of bodice. It was little more than a sleeveless vest for the peasant woman, which was cut in a deep scoop or square neck and was made without ornamentation. It laced up the front and was cut high enough and fit tightly enough to support the breasts, but offered enough freedom of movement so that she could do her work.

The middle and upper class lady's bodice covered more of her torso than the peasant's. It was made with a low, square neck or a high neck with a tall standing collar, depending on the weather, activity, modesty, prevailing fashion, or whim of the wearer. The sleeves were laced into or sometimes sewn into the armhole, and the bodice hooked or laced either up the front or the back. The fashionable bodice line for the upper class lady was flat and smooth without any bulges or wrinkles in it, and was usually worn with a corset, laced so tightly that it restricted her movements. But then, a lady was not expected to lead as active a life as a peasant woman.

Peasant, middle class and noble bodices

Basic Bodice

To make a woman's bodice, you will need a vest pattern that fits, or a high necked, tight fitting dress pattern with a waist seam. See the pattern for examples of pattern types. Folkwear pattern numbers 123 and 126 are just about perfect as they are. The first one, the Austrian dirndl should be used in the higher necked version only. The second one has several views, one even has a small peplum or skirting. A regular woman's suit vest pattern will need to be altered slightly.

You will also need fabric, lining, and medium to heavyweight interfacing, so that the bodice will hold its shape, and yours. The peasant bodice fabric hardly ever matched the fabric of any of her other garments, so don't even try. This will be a good opportunity to use up that spare yard of fabric you have had lying around for so long. Middle class and upper class bodices should match the fabric of one of the skirts, preferably the outer one.

Making a peasant bodice pattern from a modern vest pattern is relatively simple. Most of the changes are made in the front piece, because that is where the line differs. The back is much the same. The neck of the vest should be changed from the 'V' to a scoop or square cut. The darts should be left off altogether and the sides cut in more to compensate. The pattern should be cut off or folded back along the center front line for the lacing. To make the pointed waist, extend the line down the center front until it is as long as you will want it, usually about 4". Then draw a curved line from the side seam $\frac{1}{2}$" below the waistline, to the bottom of the point. On the back piece, eliminate the darts as before, and draw a line across the back $\frac{1}{2}$" below the waistline. Fold up or cut the pattern along this line. If you want, you may cut the neck down in the back a little.

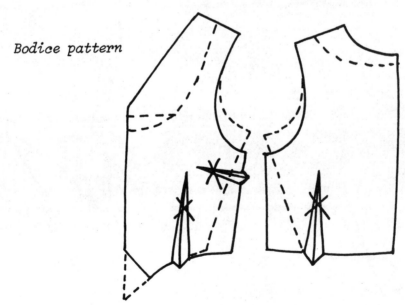

Bodice pattern

We suggest that you make a mock-up out of heavyweight interfacing to check your pattern alterations and make sure the pattern works. Just cut it, sew the seams together, make casings
down the center front to slip boning into temporarily, and punch
holes for the lacing and try it on, with the seams on the outside. Have a friend check the fit and make marks directly on
the mock-up, so that you can make any necessary changes. It
should fit snugly, without gaps or lumps. The opening in the
front should just meet, or gape slightly. Make the corrections
indicated and try it on again. Perfect? This is now your pattern.
Aren't you glad you made your mistakes on this, instead of your
more expensive fabric? We have found that beginning and intermediate seamstresses have a much smoother time if they take the
extra time to do this.

You may also want to allow a 2" seam allowance up the back
pattern piece and split it into two pieces, instead of cutting
it on the fold. This will make one more area that can be adjusted
since the underarm seams should always be approached with caution
when doing radical alterations.

To construct the vest, cut the front and back pieces out of
your fabric, lining and interfacing. Sew the pieces of interfacing to the inside of the fabric pieces. Then sew the front to
the back at the side seams, leaving the shoulders open for now.
Do the same for the lining. Then, with the right sides together,
sew the fabric to the lining, leaving an opening at the center
back along the bottom, large enough to turn the vest right side
out again. Clip all the curves, turn and press.

Before you stitch up the opening you left in the back, use
it to insert the boning in the front next to the front edges of
the vest. Sew along the edges, anchoring the boning in place,
then put in grommets next to the boning. Sew up the back opening
by hand, finish the raw edges of the shoulder seams, and sew them

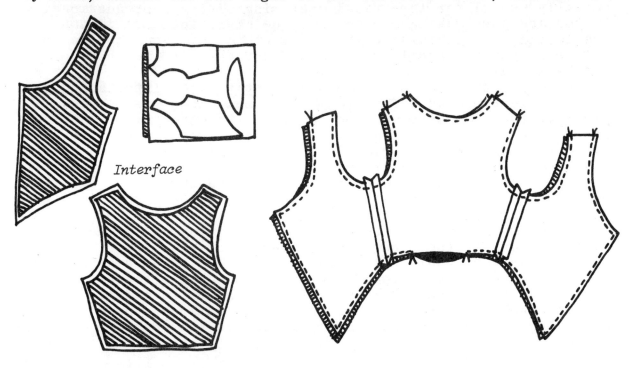

Interface

Before you stitch up the opening you left in the back, use it to insert the boning in the front next to the front edges of the vest. Sew along the edges, anchoring the boning in place, then put in grommets next to the boning. Sew up the back opening by hand, finish the raw edges of the shoulder seams, and sew them shut by hand or machine. The peasant bodice is done.

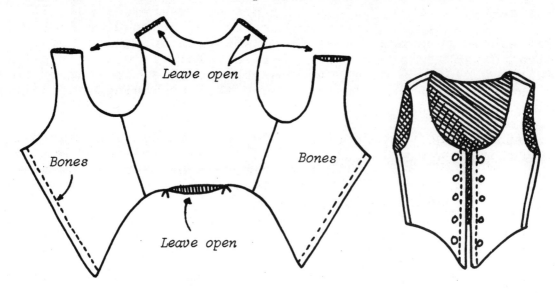

Theatrical Bodice

We have also experimented with a more theatrical approach to putting together a bodice. This method allows for more size adjustments, so that one bodice may be able to span three different sizes. It can also be put together factory-style, so even twenty bodices can be constructed at the same time. This is especially useful for theatrical costuming of large productions. If you are just making one bodice, the advantages are if you are losing (or gaining) weight, or want to loan your bodice to a friend, you can easily make the adjustments in the shoulder and back seams.

To construct the bodice this way, stitch the interfacing to each fabric piece as before. Sew the front piece to the back piece at the side seam. Do the same for the other side, but do not sew the two halves together at the back seam. Repeat for the lining pieces. With the right sides together, sew around the arm-hole, neck, down the front and around the bottom to the back. If you are going to put tabs or picadils around the waist, put them on before you sandwich the fabric and lining together. Clip the curves, turn right side out through the back you left open, and press. Slip the boning through the back opening and stitch it in place next to the front edge. Zig-zag, overlock or otherwise finish the shoulder and back edges. Then sew a seam up the back, sew the shoulder seams, and tack the seam allowances to the lining so it won't flap. Put in your grommets and it is done.

If, when you put it on, or loan it to someone, there is still a fitting problem, you can easily adjust at the shoulder and back seams.

110

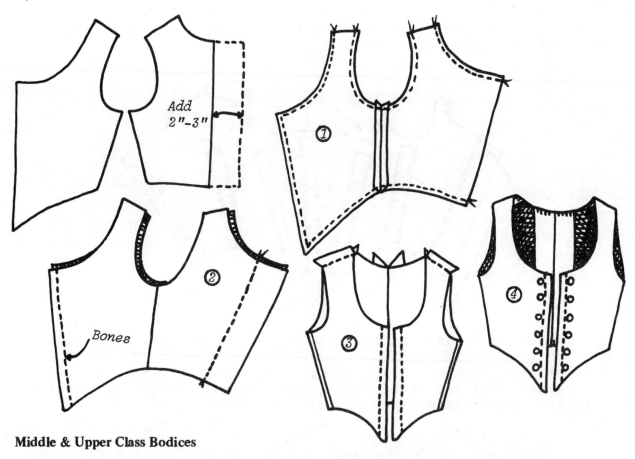

Middle & Upper Class Bodices

For a middle or upper class bodice, you can use the peasant bodice pattern with a few changes, or you can use an altered dress pattern, as described later in this section. If you intend to add tied-in sleeves, the armhole will need to be cut a little smaller. Leave out the darts as before, cutting the sides in a little bit to compensate. The bodice can be fastened up the front or the back as desired.

If you want the bodice to lace up the back, cut the front piece with the center front on the fold of the fabric and add a seam allowance to the center back edge.

The directions for constructing the bodice are the same as for the peasant bodice, with epaulets, tabs, or shoulder rolls being sewn into the armhole by hand after the shoulder seams are sewn. If the bodice will be fastening up the back, you will need to turn under the back edges about 1" and sew two pieces of boning into the back edges instead of the front edges. If you are lacing the bodice up the back or front, rather than using hooks and eyes or other fastenings, remember to sew a placket behind the grommets, so that nothing will show if the lacing gapes a little.

If you are going to be lacing the bodice up the back and will be wearing it over a corset, add a small triangular pocket to the inside of the front point. When dressing, tuck the point of your corset into this pocket to keep the bodice from riding up. If you put on your corset over you skirts instead of under them, this will keep them from shifting around, and you can tuck the corset point into the bodice pocket to keep the bodice in place as well. So clever.

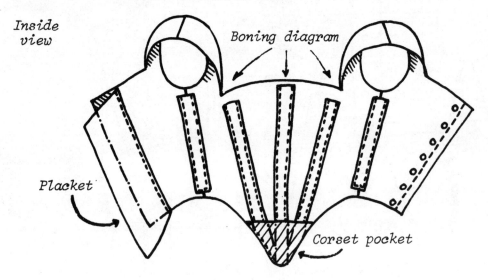

Inside view

Boning diagram

Placket

Corset pocket

If you don't want to use a vest pattern to make your bodice and you have a high necked, tight fitting bodice pattern with a waist seam, you can adapt the pattern to your purposes.

Illustrated are three basic types of modern bodice patterns, with the adaptations drawn on with dotted lines.

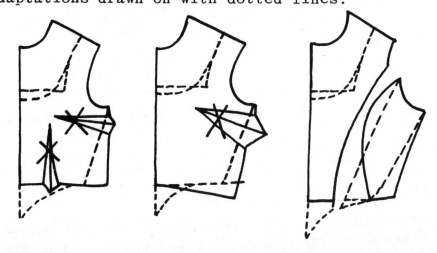

These changes are made to give a more period look to the bodice pattern, and the front darts are eliminated to give the bodice a better fit over the bust-flattening corset. This means that a corset will have to be worn.

Lady's Doublet

To make a high-necked bodice, a very common Elizabethan style, you should not cut the high neckline down, but leave it as it is, and add a standing collar, made like the neck of the shift, with a straight piece or a draped piece of fabric, lined and interfaced to stiffen it. Also, cut epaulets, tabs, or shoulder rolls if you want them and assemble according to the instructions shown earlier.

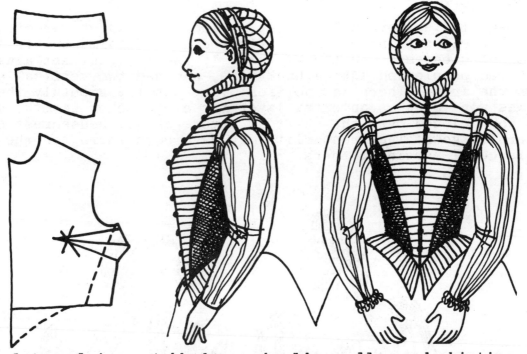

Epaulets, plain or tabbed, or shoulder rolls, and skirting pieces are the same as for the men's doublet. So follow the instructions given there for those necessary parts of a woman's bodice. The instructions for adding sleeves of various kinds are found in the sleeve section which follows.

Split epaulet & skirting   *Plain epaulet & skirting*   *Shoulder rolls & plain skirting*   *Lady's doublet with picadil epaulets & skirting*

SPANISH SURCOTE

Many ladies wore a long coat called the Spanish Surcote, or Ropa. It was a front opening, A-line coatlike garment with long or short sleeves as in the picture. It usually (but not always) gathered or pleated into a back yoke, and had two vertical slits down the front. There was no front yoke. It fit smoothly there. It was worn open as an extra layer for elegance or warmth, or was worn closed over the shift as a more casual housedress or maternity gown. The front slits may have been there for the convenience of nursing mothers.

The Spanish Surcote is a little more complicated than a plain shirt pattern, but it is not impossible. First, you need a lady's shirt pattern of the correct size. See the pattern section for suggested types. The front piece of the shirt is cut and extended as illustrated, and the back piece is cut in a slant or a curve to make the yoke. Cut a curved or slanted back body piece at least twice as wide as the yoke piece. Extend it as shown. Cut a collar, either the straight one or a draped one, and sleeve pieces, all out of the same fabric as the body.

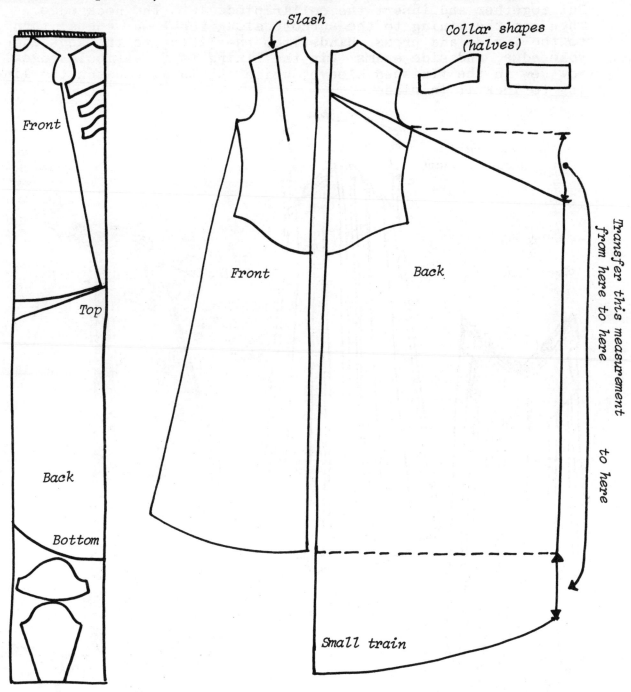

The most common sleeve that was used is like the "Queen" sleeve in the section on sleeve variations. After the sleeve is put together, it should be sewn into the armhole instead of tied in. The front pieces and the back yoke should be lined, and the yoke and front edges should be interlined, as well as the collar.

Pleat or gather the body piece into the back yoke, then sew the front and the back together at the shoulder and side seams. Sew the yoke lining and the front lining together the same way. Put together and insert the collar piece into the neck edge. Then sew the lining to the surcote along the front edges, turn to the inside and press. Handstitch the lining to the neck edge, yoke edge, and side seams. Pin the lining to the armhole edges. Now sew in the finished sleeve, which should also catch the lining to lock it in place.

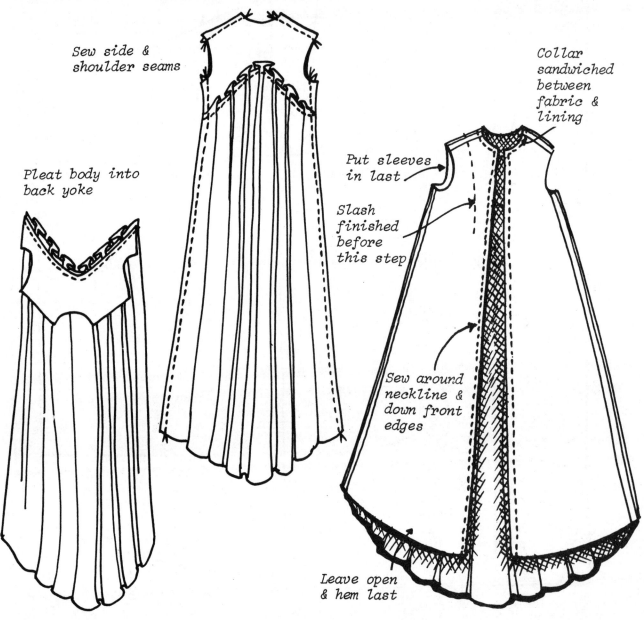

Sew side & shoulder seams

Pleat body into back yoke

Collar sandwiched between fabric & lining

Put sleeves in last

Slash finished before this step

Sew around neckline & down front edges

Leave open & hem last

If you want functional slits in the front pieces, slash the front from about 3" below the shoulder seam to about 3"-4" above the waist. Turn under the raw edges and sew the fabric and lining together by hand. Decorate the slashed edges and fasten with ties or buttons & loops. If you don't want functional slashes there, you can just sew trim to the front, where the slashes would have been and add ties or buttons to fake the fasteners.

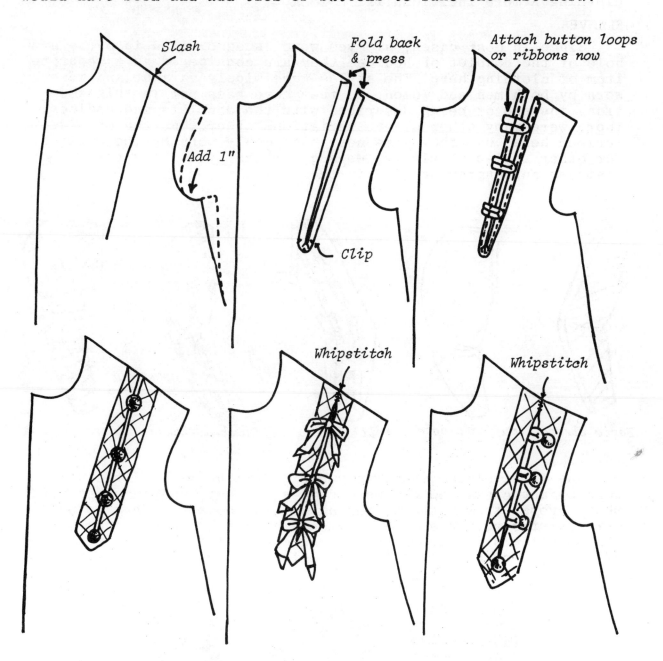

Now, decorate the collar and front edges and sew clasps or buttons with button loops along the front edge from collar to waist, and when wearing, fasten them or not as desired.

Let it hang for a few days, hem the bottom edge and the surcote is done.

SECTION IV: UNISEX CLOTHING

Many articles of clothing from this period were worn by both sexes, indiscriminately. These include sleeve variations, hats, cloaks, and other accessories. In this section, we will cover each one of these areas, and show how to give your Elizabethan clothing a more individualistic look.

SLEEVES

Since in most cases, sleeves were laced or tied into the armhole of the doublet or bodice, they are considered as a separate item of clothing here. The styles were widely variant and were worn by both men and women, so they have been put in this section, instead of being described with the doublets and bodices. There were many other sleeve variations other than the ones described here, but they were not as commonly worn by the English. For other styles of sleeve, we suggest that you check period portraiture and engravings for further details.

Basic sleeve   Stuffed sleeve   Split sleeve   Slashed sleeve   "Queen" sleeve

The first sleeve shown is a basic, plain sleeve. It can be worn by any class and may be decorated or not, as you please. We show several trim patterns throughout the book as ideas to help get you started. This type of sleeve should be lined, and makes a good pattern for undersleeves, sleeve linings for other types of sleeves, or as a base to build other styles of sleeve upon.

Basic Sleeve

To construct this basic sleeve, use a sleeve pattern from a well fitting shirt or long-sleeved dress, and cut two each from your fabric and lining. After cutting the sleeve out, add any decorations such as ribbon trim, or beading to the sleeve piece while it is still one flat piece. Then, sew the fabric to the lining along the armhole seam, turn and press. Fold in half, lengthwise and sew the long seam from the cuff end to the other cuff end. Turn the lining to the inside and sew the cuff ends together by hand, turning the raw edges under. Sew ribbon ties to the armhole edge and the basic sleeve is finished.

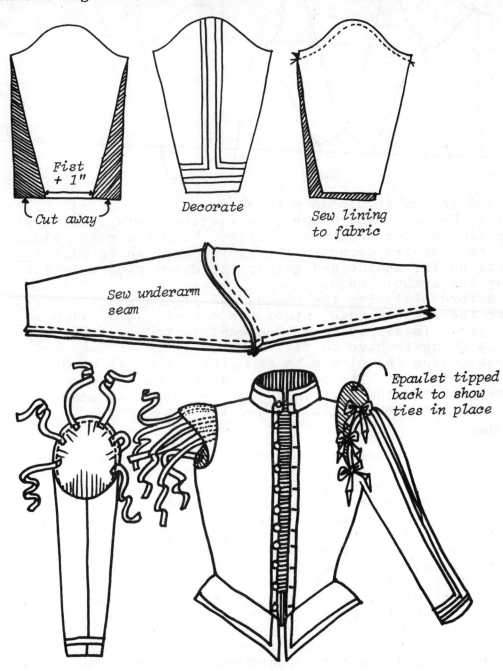

Fist + 1"

Cut away

Decorate

Sew lining to fabric

Sew underarm seam

Epaulet tipped back to show ties in place

Stuffed Sleeve

To make the pattern for the stuffed sleeve, cut the sleeve lining, using the basic sleeve pattern, then cut the paper pattern in half lengthwise. Spread the top at least 10"-12", keeping the bottom edges together. Draw a curve joining the top edges and this will be your outer sleeve pattern.

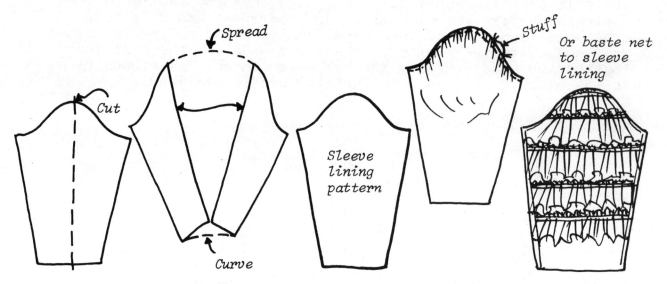

Use the outer sleeve pattern to cut your fabric and interfacing. Decorate the outer sleeve after sewing the fabric to the interfacing, but before assembling. With the right sides together sew the underarm seams in the fabric and lining pieces. Put the lining on the inside and gather the outer sleeve to the lining along the armhole edge.

Before stitching the sleeve and lining all the way closed along the armhole edge, stuff the sleeves with nylon net until the sleeve is as padded as you want it to be. Remember, your arm is going to have to fit in there later, and be able to bend. Finish sewing the sleeve to the lining and put binding around the armhole edge. Try on the sleeve and mark the cuff at your wristbone. Sew the cuff ends together with raw edges turned under. Add the ribbon ties and you are done.

Split Sleeve

The split sleeve may be cut out of the basic sleeve pattern, or the stuffed sleeve pattern. The split sleeve is usually sewn into the armhole, instead of tied in and should match the body of the garment. It may be worn over the shirt sleeve, or over an inner sleeve of some other material.

To make this type of sleeve, you should first decide which pattern you want to use. Then you you should fold the pattern in half lengthwise, then in half again. Cut the pattern along the fold line which is ¼ of the way back from the front edge of the armpit seam. Tape the pattern together along the underarm seam and this will be your pattern.

Cut identical pieces of fabric, lining and interfacing (if you are using any). Sew the fabric and lining (and interfacing) together around the front edges and cuff edge. Turn and press.

Now, decorate the sleeve if you want to, and sew it into the armhole, gathering to fit, if necessary. Sew buttons and loops, or ribbon ties along the front edges so that the sleeves may be closed in cold weather.

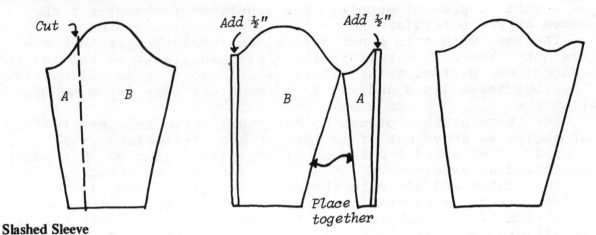

Slashed Sleeve

There are several ways to achieve the look of a slashed sleeve without the edges of the slashes raveling and driving you to distraction. Mostly, Elizabethan fabrics were more tightly woven than ours, so they had less problem with raveling edges, even when they didn't bind the raw edges, or overcast them. Also they made greater use of leather in their clothing than we do, and leather doesn't ravel.

The first method is the easiest, yet is a kind of theatrical fakery that looks best at a distance, or in circumstances where authenticity is not desired. Decide how many slashes you will want to have, and where they are going to go on the sleeve. Cut that many strips of slashing fabric (lightweight gauze, chiffon, or satin) 4" wide and 4" longer than the sleeve length. Sew each strip lengthwise and turn right side out. Lay the tubes down on the sleeve where you have decided you want the slashes to be, and choose the number of puffs that each slash will have. Baste a-cross each tube at that point and tack to the sleeve fabric, pulling it up at each stitch to make a little puff.

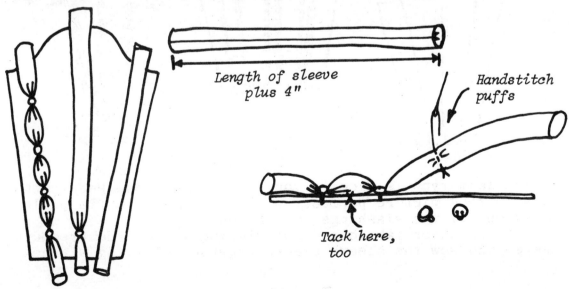

121

A button, jewel, or ribbon bow with aglets on the ends should be sewn to each point of stitching to disguise it and make it look like the fabric is poking through the fabric instead of lying on top of it. You may wish to tack the tubes all the way along the sleeve to prevent gapping. Now, continue to construct the sleeve as for a regular sleeve and it will look very good.

The next method is a bit harder, but looks better than the first one. You make a pattern for a slashed sleeve by folding the basic sleeve pattern in half lengthwise, and then in half again. Cut along these lines and add ½" to each cut edge for a seam allowance.

Use these pattern pieces to cut your fabric and interfacing. Cut strips as above out of an appropriate lightweight fabric, about 2"-3" wide and the length of the sleeve plus 4". Cut your lining and an undersleeve, using the basic sleeve pattern.

Turn under and decorate the cut edges of the oversleeve pieces, after sewing the interfacing to the fabric. Then, sew the strips of thin fabric under the edges, easing the thin fabric slightly so that it will pucker just a little and make better puffs. Pin the oversleeve to the undersleeve and sew the edges down to the undersleeve piece, pulling the thin fabric up out of the slashes as you go. Then sew the rest of the sleeve around the edges, down to the undersleeve, which will stabilize the whole structure.

Catch the slashing every few inches along the slashes with stitching and a decorative button, jewel, or ribbon tie as above. Then line and finish the sleeve as for the basic type sleeve. Finally, add the ribbon ties at the armhole and this sleeve is done.

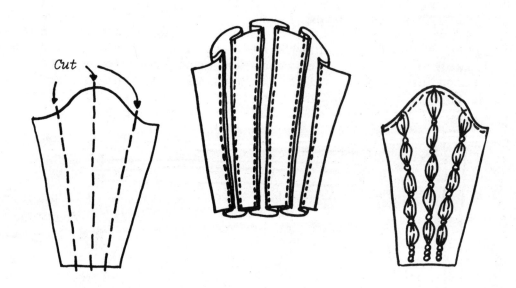

The last type is nice if you are one of those people who wants to look picture perfect, with all of your puffs pulled neatly out of the slashings, one by one.

Cut the outer fabric and interfacing as for the preceding sleeve, and sew the sleeve pieces together, leaving slashes open

as shown. Cut out 6"-8" diameter circles for each slash out of
the lightweight material of your choice. Work gathering stitches
around the edges of each circle, draw up, and pin into every
slash. Tack each securely in place, or sew around the edges of
the slash to an undersleeve. Finish the sleeve as above.

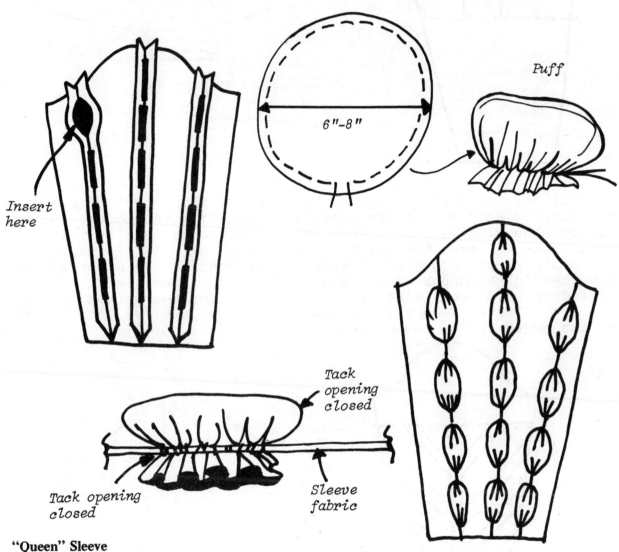

Insert here

6"-8"

Puff

Tack opening closed

Tack opening closed

Sleeve fabric

"Queen" Sleeve

The final sleeve variant shown is one which was very popular with Elizabeth, herself. She was painted many times wearing
sleeves of this type, so they are called, for the purposes of
this book, "Queen" sleeves.

To make the pattern, you must first cut your basic sleeve
pattern across, about 4" below the armhole seam and add 2" to
the top of the bottom part. This will be the lower sleeve. To
make the upper sleeve pattern you must cut the upper part of the
pattern in half lengthwise and spread it at least 10" apart at
the top and more at the bottom. Lengthen it about 3"-4" so that
it will puff out better, and draw curved lines joining the cut
edges at top and bottom. This will be the upper sleeve.

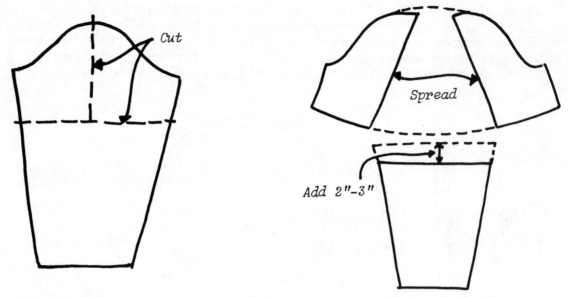

Cut the lower sleeve out of your fabric and interfacing. Cut the upper sleeve out of the same or contrasting fabric and interfacing. The sleeves can be left plain, or decorated with ribbon trim or as follows. Cut strips of ribbon or make little panes as for men's slops, about 2"-3" wide and as long as the upper sleeve. Sew them to the upper sleeve at the top and bottom edges, after the edges have been gathered to fit at the top and bottom onto the undersleeve. Decorate the lower sleeve as desired, and sew it at the edges to the undersleeve.

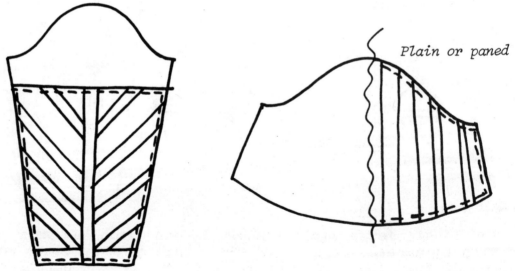

Now, lay the gathered lower edge of the upper sleeve (which has the panes or strips sewn to it) near the upper edge of the lower sleeve which is sewn to the undersleeve already.With the right sides together, sew the upper sleeve to the lower sleeve/ undersleeve combination, then flip up the upper sleeve and sew the remaining edges to the undersleeve. Before the opening is completely closed, add stuffing, so the sleeve will maintain its shape.

Then line the sleeve as described above and finish off with ribbon ties along the armhole edge. If you wish, this type of sleeve may be sewn into the armhole, instead of tied. This is a better way to do the sleeve for middle class men's doublets.

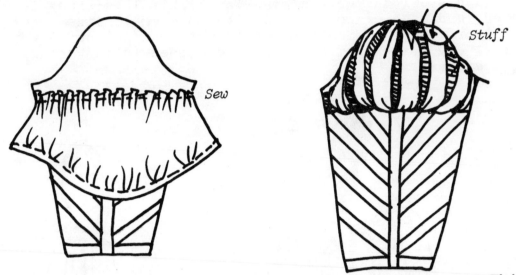

The decorative strips may be left off if you want to. This style was usually worn only by ladies with decorative strips on it, but older or middle class, conservative gentlemen sometimes wore a plain colored sleeve that was puffed down to just above the elbow, and snug from there down to the wrist. This design was a holdover from the days of Henry VIII.

LONG CAPES & CLOAKS

Everyone needed to wear cloaks or capes at some time or another. The weather got cold or wet and out would come the extra warm layers. Cloaks were almost invariably long, knee-length or longer, and made of wool lined with more wool, linen, cotton, satin, or even fur. Short capes (waist or hip length) were worn exclusively by gentlemen and are described in the men's clothing section.

Directions follow for the all-weather cloak. The easiest way to make a long cloak is to use the infinite gore pattern for skirts in the women's clothing section. This will require a fabric without a nap so that you can lay the pattern both ways for maximum fullness with the least amount of fabric.

126

Cut identical pieces out of your fabric and lining. If you want a very full cloak, simply cut more gores until you have as many as you need to get the width you want. Sew all the fabric gores together and do the same for the lining.

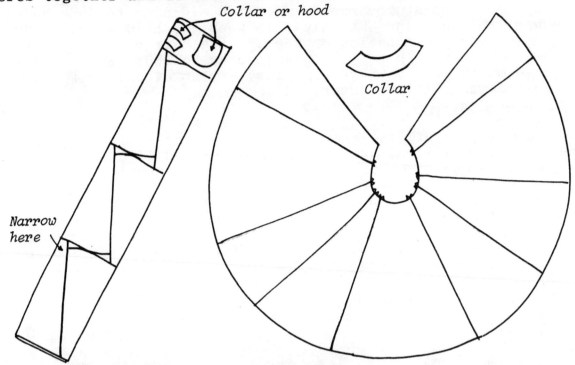

Construction of the cloak is very similar to construction of the Gentlemen's short capes. Use those directions, but pleat the body of the cape into the collar, as it is too large to lay flat. Also, commercial cloak fasteners or jumbo hooks and eyes will work on a long cloak better than ties.

If you want to make a cloak with a hood, which is practical and looks nice, the pattern is made as shown below.

Measure over top of head from shoulder to shoulder

The hood should be lined, either with the cloak lining fabric, or perhaps fur (remember the sumptuary laws). Sew the back seam in both the fabric and lining, then put the right sides together and sew around the front edge, leaving the neck edge open. Turn, press and gather or pleat the neck edge. Then proceed with the hood as if it were a collar and finish the cloak. The cloak can have a hood or a collar, but not both.

HATS, HEADDRESSES & HAIRSTYLES

Everybody over the age of twelve wore some kind of hat or headdress. This was a wise move in a country whose average summer daytime temperatures ranged from the mid 50's to 60's and rain was frequent. The hat helped to keep the head warm and dry. It also served the function of keeping the hair out of the way, of some importance in a time when regular haircuts were an indulgence of the rich. There were many styles of hat, but only the most common will be described here.

Coif

The coif, or biggins had been worn by people since the thirteenth century. It was used as an undercap and nightcap by all classes and both sexes during this period. Peasants wore it under a straw hat, mainly to keep the hair out of the eyes when working in the fields. Middle and upper class gentlemen wore it as a head warmer as much as anything else, especially the older men. During the day it was usually worn under a flat cap or a scholars biretta, a kind of squared off hat that later evolved into the mortarboard of modern times. At night, the coif would be worn as a nightcap, or a style like the crown of a bowler hat with the edge turned up would be worn instead.

The coif is a very easy hat to make. Measure your head over the top from ear lobe to ear lobe and add 4". Cut a piece of muslin this length and half as wide and drape this over your head. Starting at the center of your forehead, pin the muslin so that it fits closely over the curve of your head straight back and down to the nape of your neck.

When this feels and looks right, take it off and sew along the pinned line. After removing the pins, turn the muslin ½" back around your face until it is about 1" back from your hairline, and sew. Turn under the remaining raw edge around the bottom, until it just still covers your ears and sew it at that point. Stitch ribbons or ties at the two corners so it can be tied under the chin, and it is done.

An even easier coif or biggins that we call the Gnome Biggins takes the same rectangle of cloth and stitches it straight up the back. Hem the raw edges, sew ribbons or ties to the corners and it is done. This looks great on children. If the point bothers you, just tuck it inside and seam across the resulting triangle.

To take off point, sew here

Don't let the number of patterns presented here limit your creativity with coifs. Illustrated here are a few more ideas for you to experiment with.

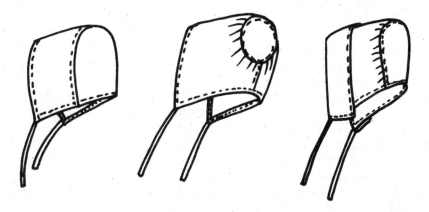

For an older gentleman, the coif or biggins can be made from a dark material instead of muslin, with black being the most appropriate, sober and respectable as it is. For a lady, it can be made of the same fabric as her gown and be richly embroidered and edged with lace, or it can be made entirely out of lace strips sewn together, if the lady is rich enough.

Draped Cloth

Lower and middle class women often used the coif to pin large squares or circles of starched linen to, in order to create their own kind of headdresses. This kind of hat was especially popular in Holland, where it still survives as the little "Dutch Cap" worn with the national costume. A couple of simple draped styles are shown here.

Front

Side

Front

Side

The second style uses a square of the same fabric 24"-28" on a side. This is folded diagonally and pinned at the center front of the coif. The ends are pinned at the nape of the neck and the top layer is folded forward until it comes down onto the forehead in a point. It is similar to the first type, but has a different final effect, because this one uses a square rather than a circle. Both the circle and square can be edged with narrow lace, if your character is well off, or makes her living as a lacer.

The first style uses a 30"-36" circle of fairly crisp finish, permaprest fabric in white or cream color to simulate starched linen. The circle is hemmed around the edge, then folded in half, then the straight edge is folded back 3"-4". At this point, it is pinned onto the coif at the center front and the bottom corners are pinned together at the nape of the neck. The top layer is then lifted up at the back, folded forward, and pinned to the top of the head (the coif, really).

Attifet

Another kind of undercap worn by all classes of women was the attifet, named after the wired front edge which could be bent into a variety of shapes around the face. Mary, Queen of Scots wore this type of cap almost exclusively, usually with a lace-edged veil over it. Its heart shaped front was very flattering to her face.

This kind of cap is a little more complicated to make than the biggins, but looks so pretty, that it is worth the extra work. We suggest that you mock this cap up out of muslin or other cheap fabric until you manage to find the exact size and shape that will look best with your face.

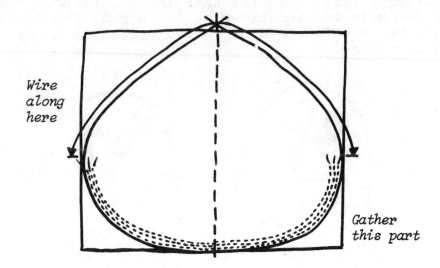

Wire along here

Gather this part

Start with a piece of fabric about 16" by 20", and using the diagram as a guide, cut a fat teardrop shape out. Sew two rows of gathering stitches around the wider curved edge. Then turn under the other edge twice, leaving enough room to insert a piece of wire through it. This part will be at the front of the cap around your face. If it is within the class of your character, you can finish the wired edge with narrow lace.

Now, pull up the gathering stitches and put the cap on your head to test where the stitches should be tied off. We cannot

131

suggest a length, as the right length will be different for each person. When it looks right to you, tie off the gathering stitches and bind the raw edge in back with a self colored strip of fabric.

The attifet can be worn under a plain or lace edged veil, or perhaps a fancy draped one, as described later. It can also be worn under the "windsock" hat or the French Hood. If desired, you can wear it by itself, as a type of indoor cap.

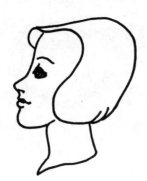

Muffin Cap

The muffin cap was called that because of its resemblance to a freshly baked muffin. It was a housewive's cap, made like a modern chef's hat, using a large circle of plain white linen or muslin gathered into a stiff brim. But, instead of wearing it on top of the head, the brim was draped over the front of the hair, and the gathered part, with the hair inside, flopped back onto the neck. The brim was sometimes cut straight, and sometimes came to a point over the forehead or curved around in a way flattering to the woman's face.

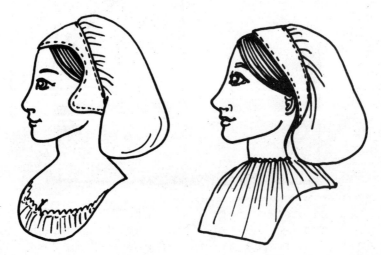

The top of the muffin hat is a circle 20"-24" across, and the plain brim is a piece of fabric 6"-8" wide and the head measurement plus 2" long. Sew the ends of the brim together, then fold it in half lengthwise. Then gather the circular part into the raw edges of the brim, zig-zagging the edge to keep it from raveling. The sewn edge will be on the inside when the hat is worn.

To make the muffin hat with the shaped brim, cut a pattern from a piece of paper 4"-5" wide and 24" long. Play with the shape of the brim, until it pleases you and use this as a pattern to cut two brims out of your fabric (and interfacing if you want to make it keep its shape). Join the ends of the brim and sew them together along the front edge. Turn and press, then finish as with the other type.

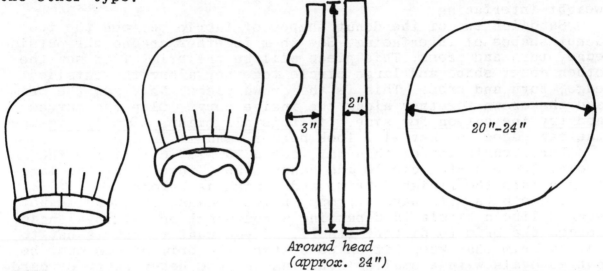

Around head
(approx. 24")

Escoffion or Caul

Similar to the muffin cap was a headpiece known as the caul or escoffion. It was made in a way similar to the muffin cap with the plain brim, except that the fabric was much richer and highly decorated with embroidery and beadwork, with a fancy jeweled headband. It should be made slightly smaller than the actual muffin cap, so that it won't hang down the back of the neck so far.

To make a caul, cut a band like that of the plain brimmed muffin cap, and a circle of 18"-20" diameter. Any decoration of the round piece should be done while it is still flat. Then, gather it into the band as for the muffin cap and decorate the band to please yourself.

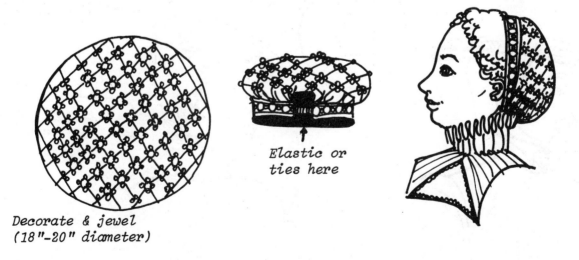

Decorate & jewel
(18"-20" diameter)

Elastic or
ties here

Flat Hat

The flat hat is very easy to make and was the type of hat most commonly worn by most classes of men and women above the rank of peasant. The flat hat requires about a yard of fabric and a simple pattern. Cut four circles with a diameter of 12". Cut a 6½" circle out of the center of three of the large circles. Then, cut two donut shapes the same as the others out of heavy-weight interfacing.

Sandwich two of the donut shapes of fabric between the two donut shapes of interfacing. Sew them together around the outside edge, turn and press. This piece will be the brim. Then sew the other donut shape and large circle together along the outside edge, turn and press. This is the crown piece. Now, sew the brim and the crown together along the inside curve. Clip the curves and try the hat on for size. If it is all right, closely zig-zag the raw edges so they will look better, and it is done.

For a variation of this hat, cut a 20"-24" circle for the crown, instead of a circle and donut shape, then pleat the large circle into the finished brim, and finish as before.

These hats will have a floppy brim, because the head is not shaped like a circle, and putting a round hat onto an oval head forces the brim to distort itself. If you want to have a hat to have a brim that keeps it shape better, the brim pieces must be cut as ovals with a smaller oval inside. Use heavy paper or card-board until you get the shape and size right, then use this for your pattern. You can also sew horsehair braid to the brim piece's outside edge before turning it right side out. Or you can insert a piece of heavy wire, such as coat hanger or millinery wire into the edge of the brim after turning it right side out.

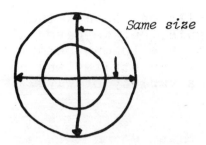

Same size

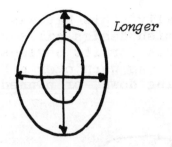

Longer

Biretta

The hat that was worn by scholars was called a biretta. This was the ancestor of the modern mortarboard hat. It was always made out of black fabric, preferably wool, velvet or velveteen, and would be worn with a black coif or biggins underneath.

The biretta is easy to make. The directions are given for an average sized head, about 23"-24" around. Take a square 20" on a side and cut off the corners so that you have an octagon with equal sides. Then cut a headband or brim piece that is 24"-25" long and 4"-5" wide.

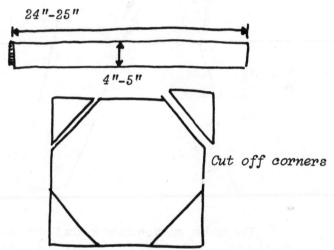

24"-25"

4"-5"

Cut off corners

To sew it together, match points B and C together, pin and sew. Do the same for D and E, G and F, and H and A. This will complete the crown piece. Sew the ends of the brim together, turn and fold in half lengthwise. Sew the crown piece to the brim, easing or stretching the square as necessary to fit the brim. Now you can finish the raw edge where the crown and brim meet with zig-zagging or binding. You can line or interface the crown of the biretta if you wish, but the hat should be a little floppy.

Join here

Finished hat

Windsock Hat

Naturally, this hat was not really called a "windsock". It was a Flemish design called the Beguin, but we have called it the windsock for its obvious resemblance to one before it is draped. It was worn over a biggins or an attifet and could be worn hanging down, or pinned up in a variety of ways.

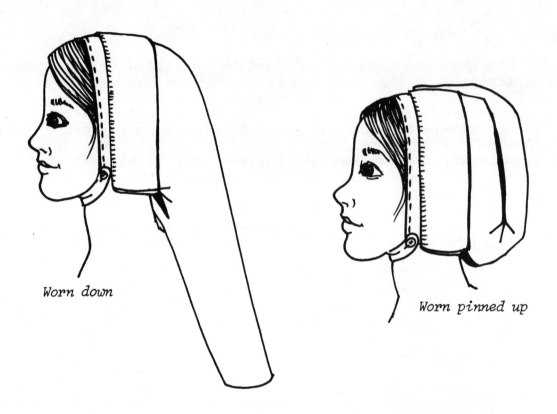

Worn down

Worn pinned up

To make a windsock hat is simplicity itself. First, cut a rectangle of fabric about 18" wide by 30" long. This can be made to match your gown or be plain white or cream color. You may cut a lining too, if you wish, but the instructions are for the easier, unlined hat.

Fold the fabric in half lengthwise with the right sides together and taper the long edge from about 8" away from one end all the way to the other end, so that the back edge will be about 12" wide instead of 18" wide.

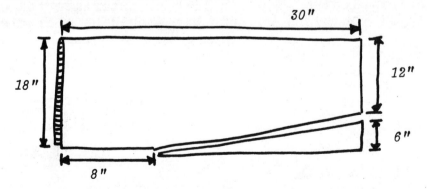

Cut a piece of heavyweight interfacing 3" by 18" and sew it to the wrong side of the fabric at the front edge. With the fabric still folded lengthwise, sew along the long edge from the point where you began to taper it, all the way to the back edge. Then fold the front edge 3" back to the outside so that the interfacing strip shows and sew each side from the fold to the edge 3" in from the fold. Turn the front right side out and press, then stitch by hand or machine, the edge which is now turned to the inside. Lastly, turn under the remaining raw edges on the sides and back edge and stitch. See - it really does look like a windsock.

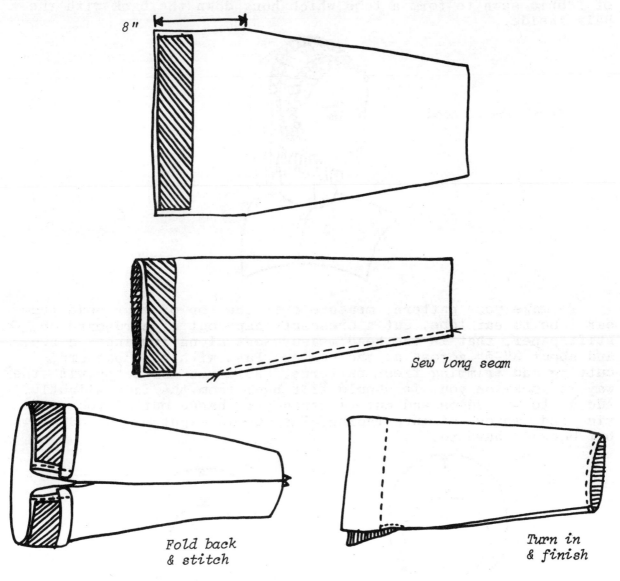

8"

Sew long seam

Fold back
& stitch

Turn in
& finish

The front edge of the hat can be wired or not as you please. Fancy decoration is optional. To wear this hat we suggest that you put on a biggins first, then pin the hat to the biggins, and stand in front of a mirror while you experiment with different draping techniques, until you find something that pleases you. If you want to, you can wear the windsock hat over an attifet instead of a biggins.

Basic French Hood

The French Hood was a common style for middle and upper class ladies throughout Elizabeth's reign. It had been fashionable since late in Henry's reign, having been brought to England from the French Court by Anne Boleyn and her contemporaries. It was basically a very simple hat that flattered almost every face.

In its simplest form, it consists of a decorated crescent shape tilted back from the face, with a veil sewn to the back. The veil was sometimes semi-circular, and sometimes a rectangle of fabric sewn to form a tube which hung down the back with the hair inside.

Simple French hood

To make your pattern, measure over the top of your head from ear lobe to ear lobe. Cut a crescent shape out of cardboard or stiff paper, that is the head measurement along its inner curve, and about 3"-5" across at the center. Fuss with this pattern, cutting and trimming fresh patterns, until you are happy with the way it looks on you. It should tilt back from the face slightly. Add ½" to all edges and cut two crescent shapes out of your fabric, and two out of interfacing. The fabric might match your gown but doesn't have to.

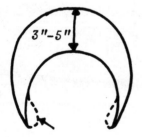
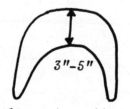

Alternate pattern

Sew all the pieces with right sides together, around the outside edge, turn and press. Put a wire, with the ends turned back, along the outer edge on the inside, and stitch into place. Turn under the raw edges on the inner curve and stitch together neatly. Now, you can decorate the French Hood as you wish and sew ribbons or ties at the points to hold it on your head.

138

For the veil, cut a half circle with a diameter of about 24" out of lightweight satin, gauze or chiffon, and hem the edges. Sew the veil to the inner curve of the French Hood from point to point and let it hang down the back of your head. You can sew beads or little pearls to the semicircular edge if you like. For this type of veil, the hair should be put up in a net or caul, or be worn in a style up off the neck.

For a tube-type veil, cut a rectangle of the lightweight fabric 24"wide and 27" long or longer. Sew the short side to the inner curve from point to point, matching centers, and then sew the long side together. Hem all the raw edges, and when wearing this, you may let your hair hang down inside the tube, if you want to.

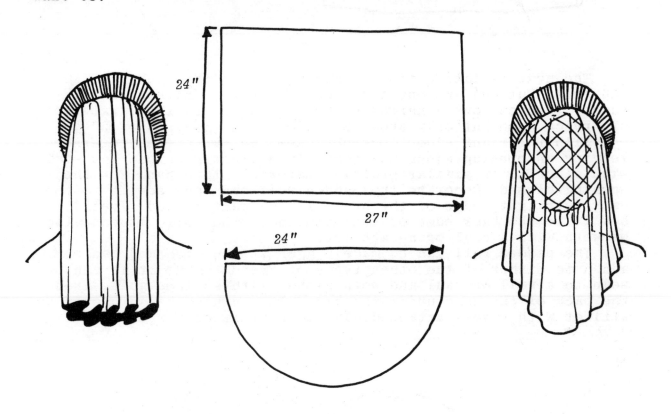

French Hood Variations

There were many variations of the basic French Hood worn by women of the middle and upper classes.

The first variation has a differently shaped piece which causes it to sit closer to the head and curve around the face more. As with the first type of hood, practice with a cut out piece of cardboard or very stiff interfacing until the shape pleases you, then use that for your pattern.

This type is constructed like the other French Hood and must be wired along its edges to make sure that it maintains its shape around the face. It can be worn with a veil or a caul. It can also be placed over an attifet with a veil behind.

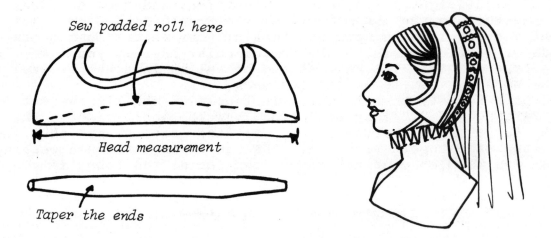

Sew padded roll here

Head measurement

Taper the ends

The next variation adds a padded roll to the fancy muffin cap brim. Cut out and put together the brim, finishing all the edges. Then cut out a narrow crescent shape like the first type of French Hood but only about 2" wide across instead of 3"-4".

With the right sides together, sew the two pieces together, leaving an opening along one edge. Turn right side out and stuff with fiberfil or similar stuffing material, then hand sew the opening closed. Decorate the padded roll and hand sew it to the back (straight) edge of the brim. If you want to add a veil, sew it to the back edge of the brim under the roll. It can also be worn with a caul or an attifet.

The padded roll can be made bigger if you wish and can be added to either of the other types of French Hood, or it can be sewn to a veil or caul and worn alone, with strings going around the back of the head under the hair. It can also be worn over an attifet with a veil attached. The possibilities are endless.

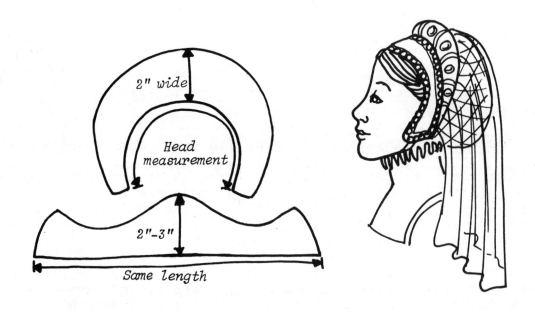

2" wide

Head measurement

2"-3"

Same length

Tall Hats

This type of hat is called a tall hat, even though it was not always tall. This kind of hat is the one pictured most often on middle class men and women during this period. It can be made with a tall or short crown, and a wide or narrow brim. Cut the hat pieces out of cardboard and experiment with them by taping them together, untaping, trimming, and retaping them until you are satisfied with the shapes and proportions.

Various styles

The first step is to measure around your head above your ears and draw an oval with that circumference plus 1". Draw another oval parallel to the first one and about 4" out from it. Cut this oval donut out and try it on your head. Fiddle with it until it looks right to you. Now, cut a 6" tall curved piece that is 2" larger than the head measurement along the bottom edge, and tapers toward the top. Tape this together, overlapping the ends, and tape it to the brim. Try it on and see if it looks right to you. If not, fiddle with it until it does. Then cut a small oval whose circumference is the same as the top opening in the crown piece of the hat. These pieces will be your hat pattern. Now untape them and trace them off onto paper so you can make another hat later, if you want to.

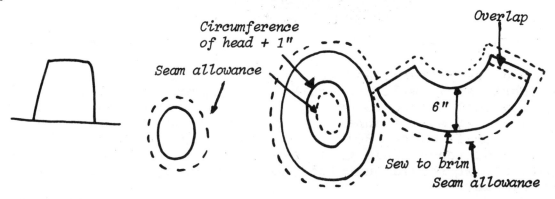

Circumference of head + 1"

Seam allowance

Overlap

6"

Sew to brim

Seam allowance

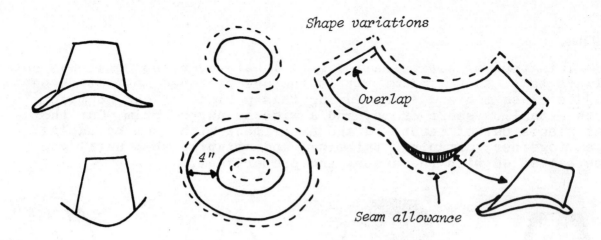

Overlap

Seam allowance

4"

Once your pattern is finished, you can make the tall hat frame from the cardboard, latch-hook rug canvas, buckram, or plastic needlepoint canvas. The disadvantage of using cardboard is that rain or sweat will warp it or cause it to fall apart, and the same goes for buckram or latch-hook canvas, which are both made of fabric impregnated with a type of water soluble startch for stiffening. If you need durability in every way, the plastic canvas will do the job for you. You can practically stomp on a hat made of this material, and it will bounce back with just a few tugs. However, the head opening should be made a little large as this material will not stretch. You can always pad the inner hatband, if the hat is a bit large when finished.

Reinforce the edges with millinery wire, coat hanger wire, or hardware wire. This can be taped on with a fabric tape like duct tape, or sewn on by hand with an overcast stitch, or by machine with a zig-zag stitch or inserted into binding sewn around the edges. Wire will strengthen the hat and allow you to bend it into a particular style. If you are using plastic canvas, which is very strong, it will need the wire to help it to stay put.

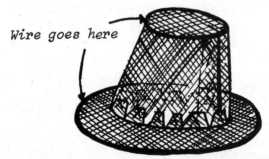

Wire goes here

When you are satisfied with the fit and look of your hat base, take your pattern and cut out the fabric cover. Make it 1"-2" larger than the pattern, and make sure that it is cut on the bias of the fabric so it will stretch over the frame smoothly. Cut out pieces of a soft fabric to use as padding over the frame. This can be two layers of soft flannel, washable felt, or very thin (1/4") foam from a craft store. Sew the padding to the frame by hand, using large stitches. This will never show, so it doesn't need to be beautiful, it should just fit smoothly and give a good base for the hat fabric.

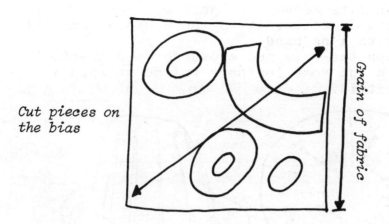

Cut pieces on
the bias

Grain of fabric

   Slit the brim pieces along the inside curve so it fits snugly
over the frame. When it is smooth, showing no wrinkles or bulges,
stitch as invisibly as possible along the outside curve. Tack into
place on the crown piece. This will be covered later. Cut out an
inner lining from the crown and top pattern pieces, and sew together by machine. Fit into place inside the hat and handstitch.
Tack the lining at the top in a few places, unobtrusively.

   Fit the crown pieces onto the frame, turning in all the raw
edges, and pin in place. Slit the crown piece edges so that it will
fit smoothly and snugly. When it is all pinned to your satisfaction, no wrinkles or gaps, slip stitch invisibly and the hat will
be ready for finishing touches.

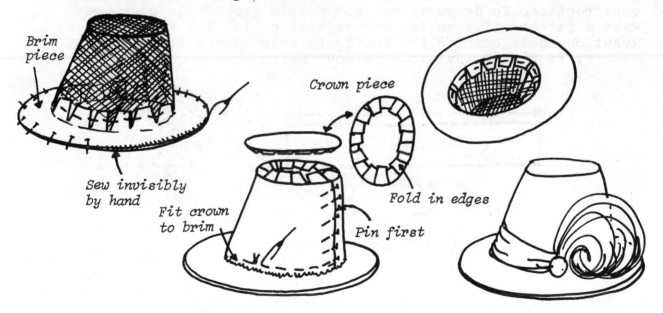

Brim
piece

Sew invisibly
by hand

Fit crown
to brim

Crown piece

Fold in edges

Pin first

   For a slightly different look, measure over the top of your
hat frame from front to back and from side to side. Cut an oval
out of your fabric that is 2" bigger than these measurements and
use this for your outer crown and top piece over the frame. Pleat
the oval in nice even pleats and pin it to the crown and top of
the frame after the brim and lining parts are finished. Trim it,

if necessary, so it fits around the join of the crown and brim, and when you are satisfied, stitch it to the crown around the bottom edge, and finish with a hatband.

Sew trim between the brim and crown for a hatband. Then attach a decorative brooch and some feathers to the hatband, if you want to dress it up a little.

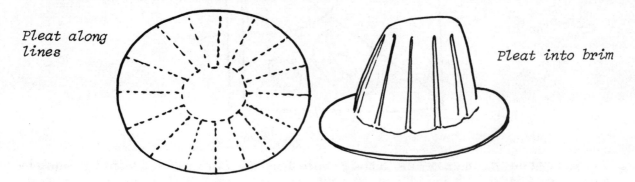

Pleat along lines

Pleat into brim

Pill Box

Another variation on the tall hat was the short-crowned, brimless hat, worn mainly in France and Italy. It resembled a modern pillbox style hat, only it was more highly decorated, of course. It was always worn far back on the head, with the hair being pulled back and tucked under it, so that it was completely covered.

You can re-cover a pillbox type hat from a thrift store, or you can make your own, using the techniques of the tall hat's construction. To dress it up, sew pearls around the edges and make a pattern of jeweling or beadwork on it. You should sew at least one hair comb to the inside to help anchor it on, or you can try to pin it invisibly to your hair.

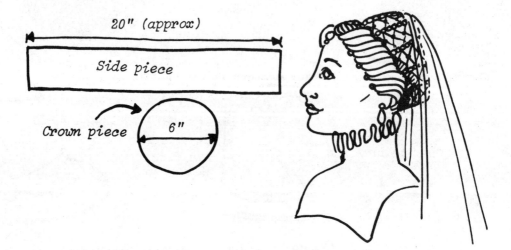

20" (approx)

Side piece

Crown piece   6"

Millinery is an exercise in patient nit-picking. The smaller and less visible your stitches are, the more beautiful and realistic your end result will be. Allow time for the handwork. A good hat will make the outfit look so much better, and a sloppy hat will detract from all your other hard work.

Straw Hats, Solanas & Wreaths

A common hat worn by peasants was the plain woven, wide brimmed straw hat, similar to that worn by farmers, even today. Rather than have you sign up for straw weaving classes at your local college, we advise you to simply buy a hat of the proper size and shape at your favorite import store. There are some straw hats coming out of China these days which look identical to pictures of sixteenth century (and earlier) peasants' hats.

These plain straw hats would be usually worn over a coif or biggins, when out of doors, and might be either tied on or be pinned to the coif to keep it on. It might have a bright colored ribbon to adorn it, or a few flowers, but it should not look like a captive garden, or a gypsy camp.

A version of the straw hat worn by middle and upper class ladies was called by the Italian name "Solana". It was tied on with a nice ribbon and was commonly adorned with a veil. It was a useful aid to Milady's complexion, and also could serve to disguise her somewhat, if the veil was more opaque and pulled over the face to hide it. This style of hat should have a wide brim and a shallow crown, another style found in many import stores fairly cheaply.

Young girls often twisted flowers and leaves into wreaths to adorn their hair during festive occasions, but seldom carried this over into everyday life, and never past the age of twenty, unless still unmarried. If you want to wear a wreath, make sure your flowers, if artificial, at least look real. After all the work of putting together a realistic period outfit, why spoil the effect with a wreath of hot pink plastic daisies.

145

Feathers

Plain or curled ostrich feathers were used extensively during this period for middle class and upper class hats. A lower middle class man might use his better's cast-offs, or wild bird feathers, to dress up his hatband. If the peasant had time to think about such things, he might use wild bird feathers, or tail feathers from his chickens.

Finding nicely curled feathers for millinery purposes is difficult, since few are being made to replenish old stocks. The techniques of working with ostrich feathers are easy, but take a light hand and patience. The tools are easy to fake. You will need a source of steam, such as a teakettle or steam iron, and a dull knife. A curling iron is nice, but not necessary. Take an untrimmed plume, as these are the least expensive, and hold it as shown.

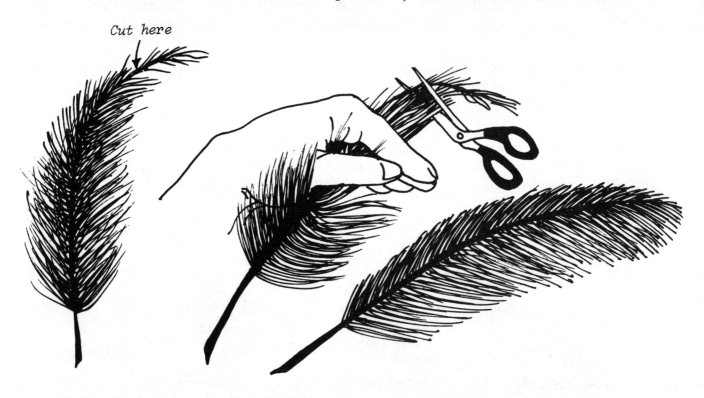

Cut here

Cut the plume straight across at the tip, after drawing it up through your fingers. When you let it go, you will notice that the feather looks fuller and nicer. Steam it for 4-5 seconds, shaking it vigorously. This will plump up the barbs. You can now curl it or put it directly onto a hat.

If you want to curl it, use a dull knife as you would curl a ribbon, but much more gently. This is laborious, but the curl is nicer than if you use a curling iron. To curl the vane or shaft, bend it carefully and repeatedly along the length of the shaft, against the knife. Work slowly and carefully, only bending it a tiny bit each time. As you work your way up the shaft, the effect will make itself more evident. This is the way all the old curled plumes were done, and with practice, your work will be the envy of your friends.

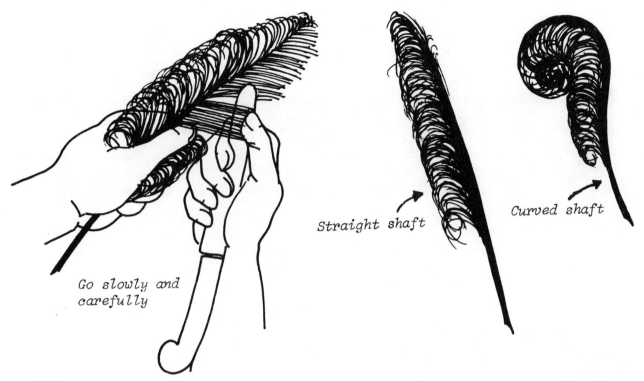

Straight shaft

Curved shaft

Go slowly and carefully

Hair

under their hats, men's hair was kept short and their whiskers were well trimmed if they could afford a barber's care. The upper classes often went clean-shaven. The lower classes were shaggier because they were combed and cut less often. See the illustrations within the text for examples.

Women's hair was usually worn long and bundled up, unless it had been cut off when the woman was suffering from a fever, or if she was so poor she had to cut it off to sell to a wigmaker, or if she had been recently in prison.

Only young girls wore their hair unfettered down their backs and uncovered by any headdress, except maybe a coif or biggins. Upper class ladies often wore wigs and false hair to augment their own, or to give them more variety in hairstyles. They also had their hair fall out, sometimes, from the rather caustic substances they put on their hair to give it the season's fashionable color.

A few styles are shown within the text and your research will show you more. You may have to look through a lot of pictures, because there are few pictures with a woman's hair showing, especially among the English.

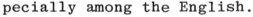

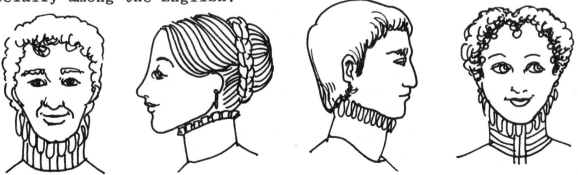

Hairstyles

RUFFS

Ruffs are what sets the Elizabethan off from any other period in history. The tiny frill at the neck of the shirt during Henry VIII's time grew so much over the next few decades, it was often removed from the shirt and treated as a separate item of clothing. The ruff was going out of fashion in England by the end of the 16th century, although it survived well into the next in the Low Countries, where it grew to millwheel proportions.

The simplest small ruff is a long strip of white fabric or lace, box-pleated into the collar and cuffs of the shirt, chemise or partlet. The rows can be doubled for a better appearance.

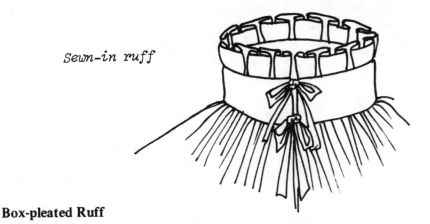

Sewn-in ruff

Box-pleated Ruff

The separate ruff can be made several ways. The easiest (and least historically accurate) method is to box-pleat a couple of rows of 4"-6" wide lace or lace-edged fabric onto a neckband made of a 1" wide ribbon as long as the neck measurement plus 1". Sew the first row to both edges of the ribbon, and sew the second row down the middle. This will give the ruff better depth. Sew hooks and eyes onto the ends of the neck ribbon and the first ruff type is done. It will fit tightly around the neck. That's all right. It's supposed to.

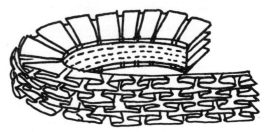

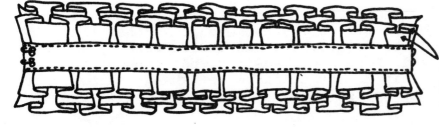

Back & front staggered in size to show pleating Both are acutally same size

Accordion Ruff

The second type of ruff is made by accordion pleating a long stiffened strip of fabric or lace onto a neckband which itself is stiffened with several layers of interfacing. The ruff fabric is best stiffened with an edging of horsehair braid sewn in one or more rows to the fabric on the inside, where it will not show. The pleats are sewn by hand to the neckband along the top and bottom edges, about $\frac{1}{4}$"-$\frac{1}{2}$" apart. When you have finished, sew hooks and eyes to the neckband. This method is tedious and time consuming, but the results will be very good if you can work with lots of patience.

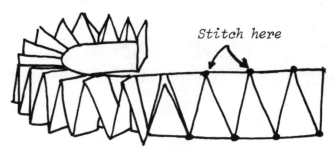

A variation of the accordion-pleated ruff is to avoid creasing the fabric as you put it on the neck band. Make sure you stiffen the ruff fabric with at least two rows of $\frac{1}{2}$" horse hair. Stitch it as before, allowing the fabric to form graceful curved folds, like candy ribbon.

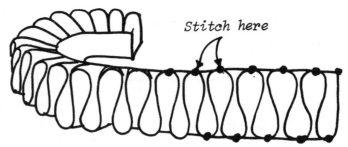

Gathered Ruff

The next type of ruff is the most complicated type, but it looks better than any of the other types, and extensive research indicates that it was one of the commoner methods of making a ruff back then.

After you have cut your strips of fabric and sewn them together into one long piece. Finish the outer edge with lace if you want it, and horsehair to stiffen it, and then sew two or three rows of gathering stitches to the inside edge and pull them up so that the piece of fabric goes into one long spiral. It should not be too tight a curve, but enough so that the outer edge of the ruff will be fuller than the inside edge. That will guarantee that you will have the classic "candy ribbon" look. Now sew the fabric strip to the collar or neckband, either by box-pleating it, or by accordion-pleating it, as you desire. Now, isn't that nice?

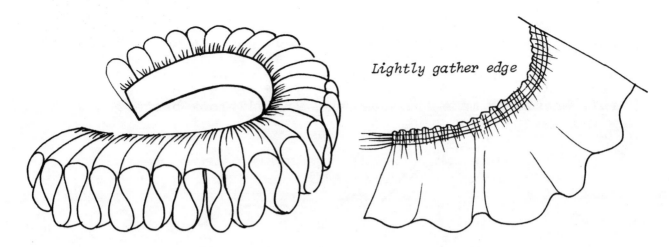

Lightly gather edge

Circular Ruff

Another way to do this is by using circular pieces sewn together so that the outer diameter is larger than the inner diameter. Draw 8-12 12" diameter circles on white fabric, and half as many identical circles on interfacing. Draw 5" diameter circles inside the first circles for a ruff that will stick out 3" from the neck when finished. Adjust accordingly for wider or narrower ruffs. Cut out all the circles, inside and out, then slash each circle.

Sew half the circles, with the interfacing attached, to each other to make a long, curved strip. Sew the other half of the circles together the same way. With the right sides together, sew the two long strips along the outer curve and ends. Then turn, press, and sew together along the inner curve with a zigzag stitch so it won't ravel. If you want lace on the edge, sew it on now. And if you want the edge to really hold its shape, sew horsehair braid along the outer edge.

Now, sew the strip to the collar or neckband as above. This method of making a ruff ensures that it will be sturdy and easy to care for. You should be able to throw this ruff into the wash with the rest of your laundry and it will come through like a champ.

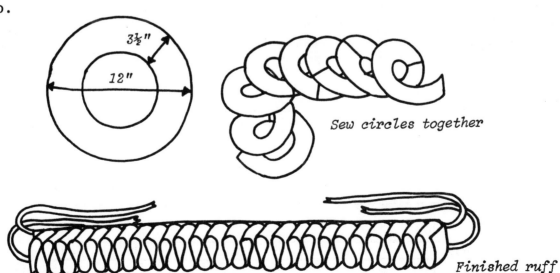

Sew circles together

Finished ruff

Wrist Ruffs

Wrist ruffs are made the same way as the different types of neck ruffs, however they should be scaled much smaller because the wrist is smaller than the neck. And you might want to be able to use your hands without 3" wide wrist ruffs hampering every move. If you make a neck ruff in one style, the wrist ruff should be made the same way. It will look better.

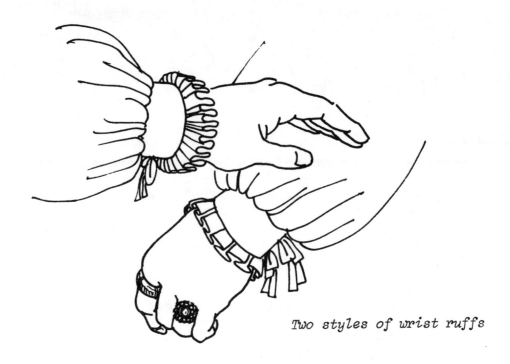

Two styles of wrist ruffs

Ruff Machine

Illustrated here is what we call a ruff machine. It was invented by Stuart White, a friend of ours, when he heard us complaining of cramped hands while doing multiple ruffs. If you are planning to make more than one set of ruffs, this contraption will make your life a lot easier.

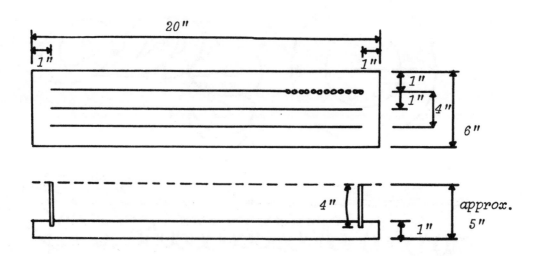

What you will need is a piece of 1X6 wood, some $\frac{1}{4}$' hardwood doweling, and access to a drill press, or one of those stands that you can use to turn your portable electric drill into a kind of drill press. This way, you can drill holes that will be exactly vertical in the piece of 1X6. Follow the plan shown. Drilling three rows of holes allows you to make both wide and narrow ruffs. Do not glue the pegs in place as you will be wanting to move them around as you go from size to size.

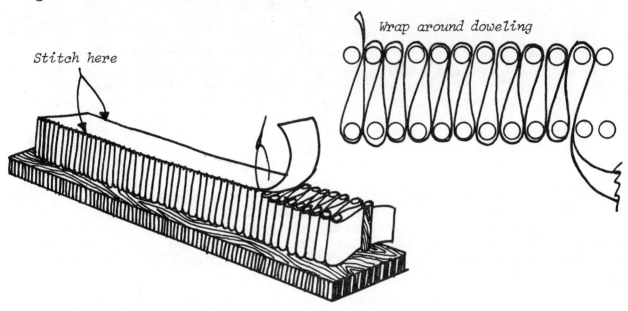

Wrap around doweling

Stitch here

LEGWEAR

Hosen

Hosen were a necessity as well as fashion for the Elizabethans. In a climate, where on a fine June morning, you could watch the ice crack on the duck pond, bare legs were almost unknown.

Hosen were usually made as separate legs and either reached to the waist, tying there, or were thigh length and were either sewn to the trunk-hose or breeches, or were held up by points tying to a belt similar to a garter belt, or a strip with eylets in it sewn to the inside of the doublet. Garters as well, were used to keep the hosen in place and smooth looking.

Hosen were often worn in layers for warmth, covering any holes with another pair, and the finest pair was worn on the outside to display them. One look among the nobles was to wear a thigh length pair over a waist length pair of a different color. The shorter pair would be held up by garters. Some boots even imitated hosen by being made of the softest kid leather, like glove leather, and worn with shoes over them. Boot-hose, made of some sturdy fabric, were often worn between boots and fine silk hose to protect them. The boot-hose sometimes showed a fine lace edging at the top of the boot, and later in the century, was folded down over the top of the boot to display that lace.

Lower class hosen were basically tight-fitting trousers with
feet attached. They were made of bias-cut fabric for stretch,
and invariably bagged and sagged, which bothered the peasant
not a whit. He had more important things to worry about.

Upper class hosen were often knitted, but bagging and sagging
were still a problem. Towards the end of Elizabeth's reign, silk
stockings became the rage, never to lose their hold on fashion
until the invention of nylon stockings in this century. The late
sixteenth century also saw the invention of a knitting machine or
frame for the easier manufacture of stockings. It was denounced
from the pulpits as the devil's handiwork.

For the purposes of this book, we will state here that for
all but the perfectionists among us, purchased dancer's tights
will do just fine. Buy them a size too large, if you want to
have that slightly baggy look at the knee and ankle. Men should
open up the front crotch seam for convenience and comfort.

If a more authentic look is desired, we have included two
patterns which are the best we have seen or used. They are from
"Costume and Fashion", by H. Norris (see Bibliography). You will
need to do a lot of experimentation and mock-ups, since every
body is different, and the hosen fit very closely.

The first of these patterns comes from a surviving pair of
hosen found in an archaeological excavation. It was probably
worn by a lower to middle class person since the fit is not very
tight. After sizing to your satisfaction, join AF to CG. Then
put in H as shown, adding the sole of J last.

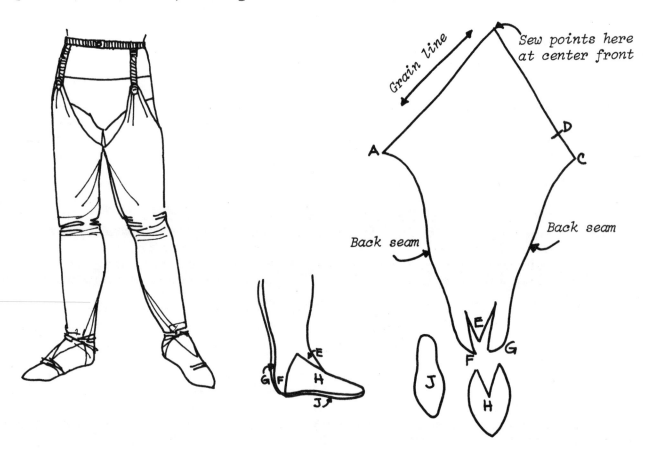

154

The second pattern is one that had been experimented with and was refined from the preceeding pattern. The measurements are for an average man with a 31" inseam. Change the proportions as needed, and make mock-ups until you are satisfied with the result, then the mock-up can be your pattern.

To make this pattern, join outside seams ABC to DEF. Join inside seams HI to RQ, leaving 8" open to be laced up when the hosen is worn (making sewn eyelets, not metal ones. This will give a little ease in the design. Sew triangular gusset PT to the leg. Then join T to N and C to M. Join NML to FKJ and you should be done. For a more modest look, you may want to include the areas marked as "overlap". These pieces will cross over in front and back when the hosen are tied on.

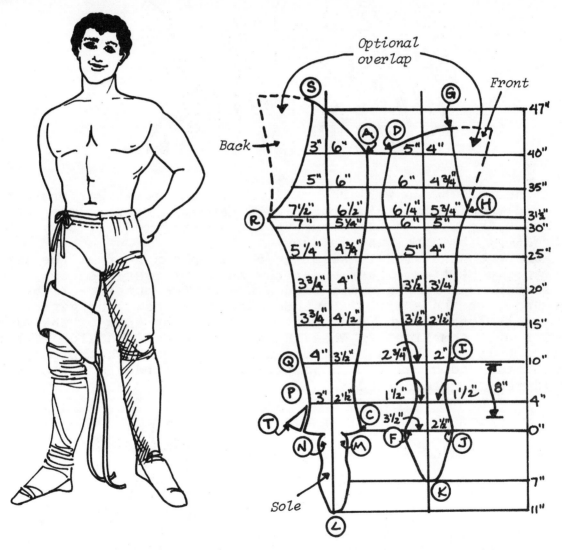

If you have gone to all this trouble to make the hosen, you should try to fasten them as the Elizabethans did. Sew several sets of points or ties to the top of each leg and thread the points through eyelet holes in the waistband of the breeches and eyelet holes in the lining of the doublet. Or sew a strip of fabric with eyelet holes in it to the doublet lining under the

the skirting, where it will not show. After you have threaded the points through all these holes, tie them together and your hosen will stay up. As a kind of bonus, your breeches and doublet will stay in place too, no matter how active you are, because you have tied them all together as one unit.

Garters

Since all hosen will bag a little at the knee, garters can be used to minimize this problem. Elizabethan garters were often fancy, being made of sumptuous fabric and trimmed lavishly with embroidery, beading, and fringes.

Garters were used to keep the hosen up and neat on the leg. They could be tied either under the knee, or over the knee, crossed behind the knee and tied again on the outside of the leg under the knee with a bow. So make sure that your garter ribbon is long enough to do what you want. The ends of the tied garter were sometimes fringed. Some garters were buckled like a little belt, around the leg just under the knee. The Knights of the Garter had buckled blue garters with the Order's motto embroidered in gold around it.

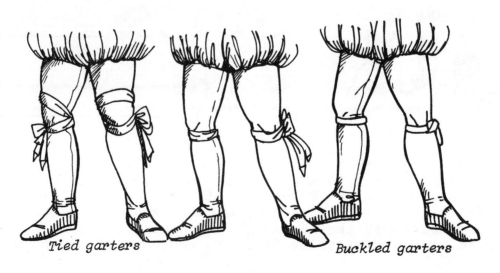

Tied garters   Buckled garters

Shoes

Shoes for peasants should be either leather "earth-shoe" type shoes, sandals, boots, or "kung-fu" style cloth shoes. There are shoes exactly like modern kung-fu shoes (except for the soles) right down to the buckle fastening, in a painting called "Peasant Dance" by the Flemish master, Breughel.

Middle and upper class people should wear loafer type shoes, low boots, or kung-fu shoes, with perhaps, decorative buckles or Shoe Roses on them.

Straps go up to belt to keep boots up

Cork sole

Satin shoe

The shoes pictured here are all taken from contemporary sources, and were worn by both sexes, with the exceptions labeled. Upper class footwear differed from lower class in proportion, materials and detailing. Sandals were worn by only the poorest folk.

People with wealth (or pretensions to wealth) often protected
their fancy, delicate slippers by wearing overshoes, called
pantofles, similar to "mules". A lady might wear chopines, which
elevated a woman so her skirts wouldn't drag in the muck of the
streets.

Pantofles

Chopines

Shoe Roses

Shoe roses were the most common method of decorating the
front part of the shoe, called the vamp. They were worn by any
man or woman who wanted to make their shoes look more fancy. Of
course, peasants had no time or money for such frippery.

Shoe roses are easy to make, requiring about 2-3 yards of
ribbon and two 2" circles of canvas or other strong, non raveling fabric. Cut 3"-4" lengths of the ribbon and fold each one
in half. Sew the ribbon loops in two concentric circles onto
the fabric circles, then sew a button in the center.

Sew the shoe roses onto the front (Vamp) of the shoe, or
poke a couple of holes in the base fabric and thread a string
through the holes to tie the shoe roses to the shoelaces (if
the shoe has any) or through holes in the top of the shoe if it
doesn't.

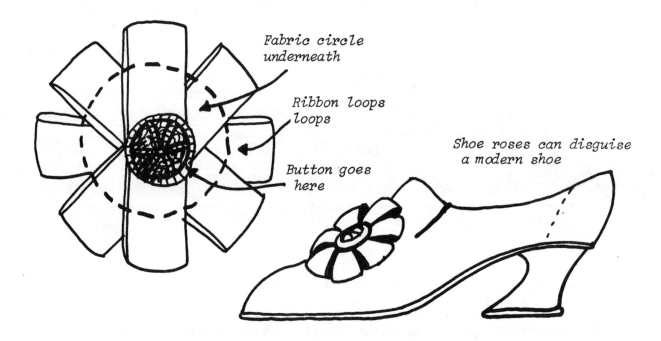

Fabric circle
underneath

Ribbon loops
loops

Button goes
here

Shoe roses can disguise
a modern shoe

ACCESSORIES

Pouches

Pouches were the pockets of the Elizabethans. They were suspended from belts and were made in many different styles out of fabric and leather. Some basic drawstring pouches and a foldover type are shown here.

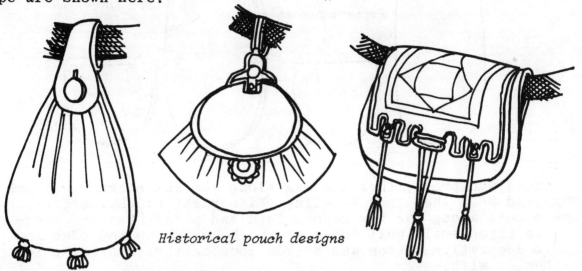

Historical pouch designs

To make a simple drawstring pouch, cut your fabric, using one of the patterns illustrated, or make up your own. Turn down the top edges of each piece to make a casing after turning under the corners. Then with the right sides together, sew around the pouch, leaving the casings free. Turn, press, and put the drawstrings through the casings and tie knots in them. If you want to decorate the pouch, do so before sewing the pieces together.

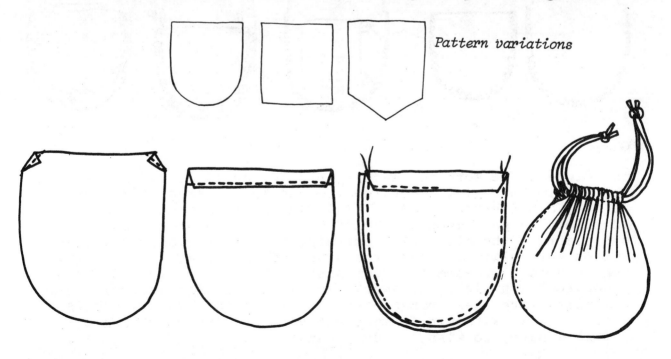

Pattern variations

For a foldover pouch, cut the fabric and lining, using the pattern pieces like the ones shown. Cut them large or small as desired. With the right sides together, sew the fabric to the lining along the lines shown.

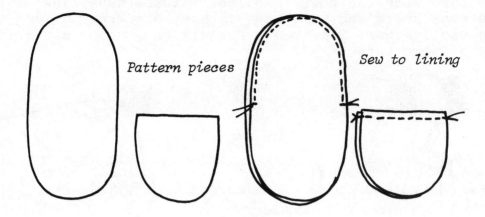

Pattern pieces   *Sew to lining*

Turn and press, then zig-zag along the raw edges to finish them and keep them from raveling. With right sides together, sew the pieces along the raw edges. Turn and press. Sew one large or two or three small belt loops at the back of the top edge and sew a decorative button and button loop on the front flap to fasten it with.

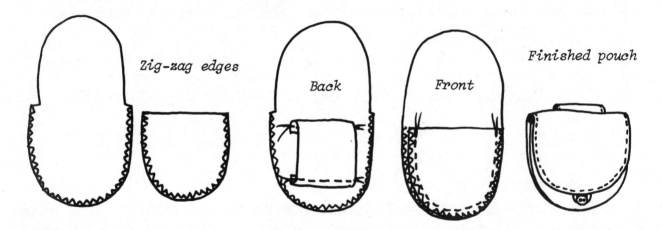

Zig-zag edges   *Back*   *Front*   *Finished pouch*

Gloves

Gloves were worn for warmth, protection while riding, and for show. The nobles decorated and scented their gloves, just as they did everything else. Plain white or colored gloves can sometimes be purchased at thrift stores for under a dollar. You can decorate the glove with embroidery, lace edging, or cuttes. Cuttes were slits cut over the knuckles and rings, so that the hand had more freedom and room inside. Leather gloves were also decorated with pinks, beadwork, and jeweling (for nobles). They sometimes wore their rings over the gloves for show, which is a clever trick, although it makes it very hard to get the glove off in a hurry to kiss a lady's hand.

Fencing gauntlets also make a very good, period-looking man's glove or gauntlet. It can be decorated with pinks and cuttes, or as the other gloves described above.

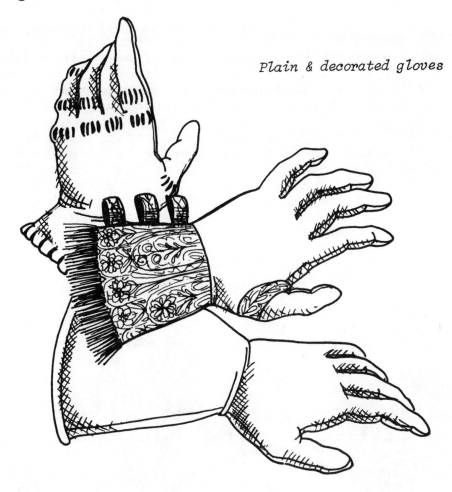

Plain & decorated gloves

Mirrors

Ladies and very vain young men wore or carried small mirrors about their persons. It might be sewn to the base of a fan, or the inside of a tall-crowned hat. Or it could be set into a frame and hung from the girdle with a cord or chain.

Pomanders

Pomanders were carried by the upper middle and upper class gentlemen and ladies. This sweet-smelling object was a wise thing to have about one, when living in cities whose streets were open sewers.

To make a simple one, stick many cloves into a lemon or orange in a pleasing pattern, and let it dry in an airy place for a couple of weeks. Hang this from your girdle or belt with a cord or put it in a decorative covering and then hang it from your belt.

We include for your information a recipe used in the 16th century for a filling used in a pierced metal pomander. "Make a pomemaunder under this manner. Take of Lapdanum iii drams, of wodde of aloes one drame, of amber of grece ii drames and a half; of nutmegges, of storax calamite of eche a dramme and a half; confect all these togyther with Rose-water, and make a ball. And this aforesayd Pomemaunder doth not onely expell contagyous ayre, but also it doth comforte the brayne" 1542. Andrew Boorde's Dyetary of Helth .

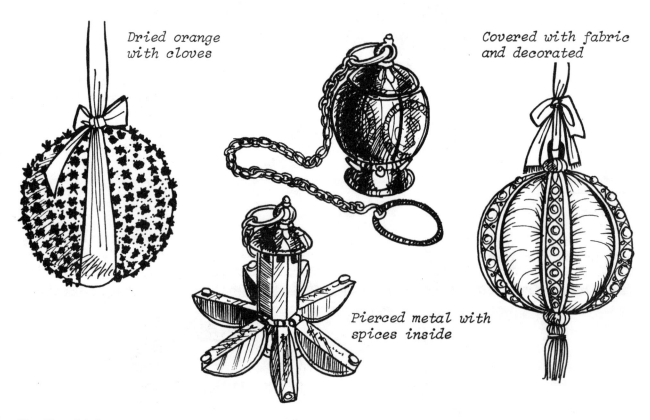

Dried orange with cloves

Covered with fabric and decorated

Pierced metal with spices inside

Handkerchiefs

Lace edged or tasseled handkerchiefs were also used by the upper classes for favors to give and keep, as well as the usual uses for a handkerchief. They were perfumed for the same reasons that a pomander was made and worn. It served to keep away "bad airs".

Masks

Many upper class ladies, or middle class ladies with pretensions, wore masks when going out in public. This guaranteed anonymity, and also served to protect the complexion from the sun and wind. The mask was usually made out of black velvet or satin in the shape of an oval, lined with kid leather or silk, and had holes for the eyes. There was usually a button sewn to the inside surface which was gripped between the teeth to hold the mask in place.

Button here

Eyeglasses

Eyeglasses of the small wire-rimmed type were known to the Elizabethans, but they were not commonly worn by any but the merchant classes or scholars. They did not have curved temple pieces, but fastened to the ears by loops. El Greco painted a Spanish Cardinal wearing eyeglasses of this type.

We suggest that, unless you can justify through your character, the wearing of eyeglasses, you just try to muddle through with contact lenses, or work the short-sightedness into your character somehow. If it is a question of personal safety, such as riding in a tournament, by all means, wear them and welcome.

Fans

Most ladies and some male dandies carried fans. The lower class fans were simple affairs made of straw and can be found, almost unchanged in design, in many import stores, at a very low price. Upper class fans were mostly made of feathers, and this type can also be found in import stores. The feather fans can be decorated on the handle and around the base, and can be hung from the girdle by a cord.

The Italians had a fan shaped like a stiff flag on a stick, and this can be made easily out of a brocade and trimmed with ribbon and beads. Folding fans, however, were mostly unknown, being introduced to Europe (England) in the 1580's.

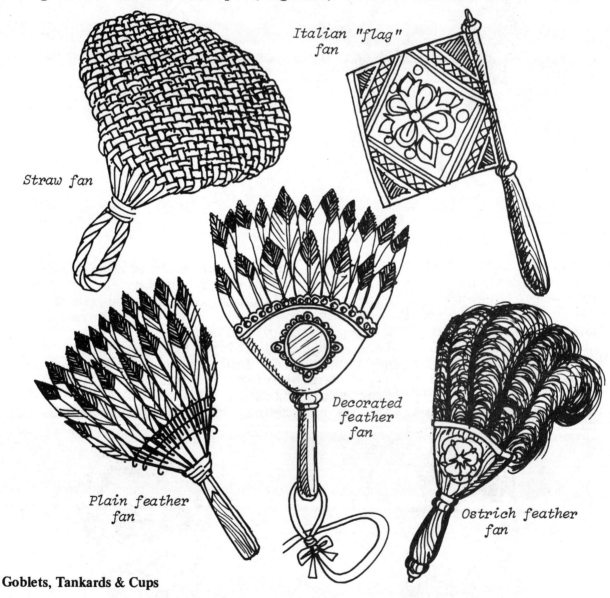

Italian "flag" fan

Straw fan

Plain feather fan

Decorated feather fan

Ostrich feather fan

Goblets, Tankards & Cups

Water, ale and wine were drunk from various types of cups, more often made of wood or metal, than glass, rare and fragile, and therefore limited to the nobility. A well-made pewter cup was considered a good dowry for a poor girl, and tankards of various types were used in every alehouse.

If you are in a situation where you feel hot and dehydrated, such as under stage lights, or at a summer festival, try to work the carrying of a goblet into your character. Put water, not beer or wine into the goblet or tankard, because any form of liquor will dehydrate you, no matter how good it tastes. You will be more comfortable in the long run, if you stick with Adam's Ale.

Many craftsmen, these days, are making fine pewter goblets, mugs and tankards. For those who prefer economy over authenticity the aluminum tankards commonly available are quite acceptable to all but the most picky. We suggest that you paint the outside of the bottom of glass-bottomed styles with metallic paint.

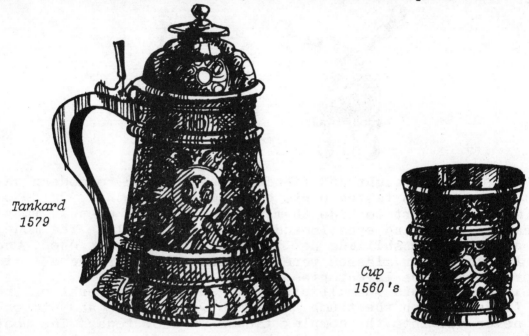

Tankard
1579

Cup
1560's

Baskets

Baskets made of woven straw were carried by lower class and middle class women to do their marketing and carry various small objects. Upper class ladies had no need of baskets to carry things. They had servants for that, after all.

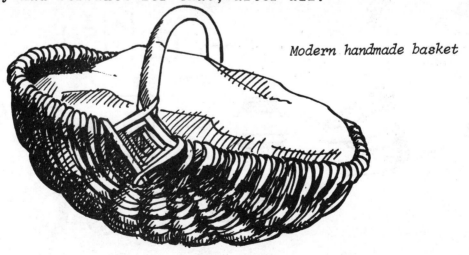

Modern handmade basket

Jewelry

There was very little in the way of jewelry available to the lower and lower middle classes. Simple bead necklaces of glass or shell were most commonly worn. Pins of various kinds were used and buttons could be ornamental. Metals used would be no finer than pewter or brass, unless stolen. Jewels set in metallic backings, such as brooches and rings, would be unknown, being much too expensive for the commonality.

As a person went up in the world, he or she might want to display their new-found wealth in the form of rings, fancy pins, gold or silver chains, buckles, or buttons, necklaces with flat cabochon cut stones, or collars of office.

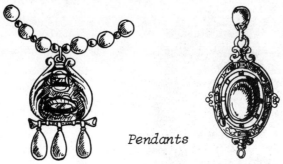

Pendants

Pins, both straight and fibula type (similar to modern safety pins) were used to fasten parts of garments together. Quite often, they made no effort to hide them, so they can be seen in many old portraits. Hooks and eyes looked almost exactly like the modern ones and cost one shilling per thousand for ordinary ones. Ones made for the upper classes were made out of silver and are listed in period wardrobe inventories.

Rings were worn in multiple sets, sometimes several on the same finger, or on the thumb. Settings were simple and stones were never cut into the complex facets we know today. The most complicated cut a stone usually had was a plain emerald cut.

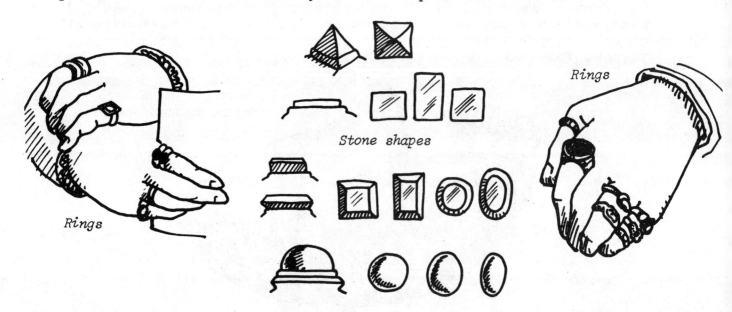

Rings

Stone shapes

Rings

Earrings, mostly of the pendant type, were worn by both sexes among the upper crust. Gentlemen usually only wore one, however. A pendant pearl was the most popular kind worn by them. Ladies wore both pendant pearl types of earrings, and stones set into precious metals, hung by a hook through the pierced ear lobe.

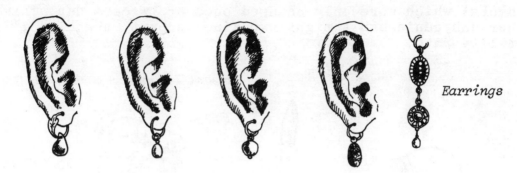

Earrings

Miniature paintings of loved ones were also used as jewelry by many people. These pictures were set in little frames or lockets and worn as necklaces or pinned on as brooches. You can simulate this by cutting out the head and shoulders part of a period portrait from a postcard (total cost maybe 25¢) Then set the little picture into an oval frame that you can find at jewelry or craft stores with a pin backing already on it. This will look very nice. Or if you have painting talent, or you have a friend you can barter with, have a little picture painted for you that will fit into one of those frames.

Some lucky noble persons might have a Nuremburg Egg, a kind of pocket watch. It was put into a case richly jeweled and was carried in the hand or worn on a chain. It was only moderately reliable as a timepiece, but it was certainly better than the alternative, which was no timepiece at all.

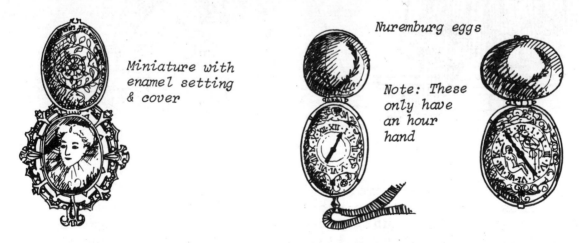

Miniature with enamel setting & cover

Nuremburg eggs

Note: These only have an hour hand

We show some examples of jewelry here and throughout the text. We suggest that you augment these pictures with some research of your own. It's fun to look at all those paintings of people who were alive so long ago, and try to imagine what their lives must have really been like.

SECTION V: CHILDREN'S CLOTHING

As we have mentioned before, most children's clothes were designed exactly like that of their parents. If you consult many old paintings and prints, you will see the truth of this.

Babies were put into swaddling clothes (tightly wrapped blankets) which were only changed once or twice a day. This rather unhygenic habit might explain, in part, the high infant mortality rate.

Peasant lad meets little lordling

When children began to crawl and walk, they were put into long shirts if they were peasants, or dresses if they were middle or upper class, until they were toilet trained..Both boys and girls were dressed like this because it made it much more convenient for their mothers to change their clouts (diapers) as necessary.

After the child was toilet trained, he or she was dressed exactly like a small adult. For practicality's sake, we suggest some changes to the adult styles.

First and foremost, use a sturdy and washable fabric and trimmings. There are few things more heartbreaking than seeing your darling urchin greet you cheerfully, after a day of play in the dirt, wearing what was this morning, a little nobleman's suit that you put untold hours of work into, and is now ruined beyond redemption.

Remember, no matter how he or she is dressed, your kid will still act like a kid! So keep this in mind when designing the clothes.

Secondly, make the clothing adjustable, if you want your child to be able to wear it more than a few times. Children grow so fast (inconsiderate of them, don't you think?). Make deep hems on sleeves and skirts, and fasten the clothes with lacing with a wide placket behind them for adjustability. Make great big seams that can be let out later.

Next, children are prone to lose things if given half a chance, so keep removable parts to a minimum. Sew the girl's bodice and skirt together. Sew in the sleeves or tie them in with knotted ribbons (toddler ties), so they cannot be readily undone by small fingers. Tie on the hat, or pin it to the coif or biggins which itself is tied on securely.

A simple variation from the adult bodice and skirt combination for peasant and lower middle class girls is shown below. It looks reasonably historically accurate, comfortable to wear, and very easy to make and alter as she grows. It is most suitable for the 2yrs-10yrs crowd. After that, she will really want to dress more like an adult.

Over the shoulder measurement

Shoulder strap

Chest measurement

Bodice piece

4"-6"

Chest to floor measurement

Make the overdress out of a sturdy, medium weight, washable fabric. Cotton is best, or a linen-look fabric. Or you may want to use a washable well-textured drapery fabric. Allow for generous hems in the overdress and the shift beneath. The girl is going to grow up faster than she will grow out, so the front lacing should be suffient for growth out and the deep hems can be let down as necessary for growth up.

The last point we want to make about children's clothes is to keep it simple. Save the fussy little details for someone who can appreciate them properly. Children's clothes are smaller than adult's clothes and can be left fairly plain and still look just fine. And children, no matter how they are dressed, are going to run you just as ragged, so why not relax and enjoy it.

Peasants have the most fun.

"Wanna play?"

APPENDIX

NOTES ON NEEDLEWORK

The Renaissance, both in England and on the Continent, was a return to the purity of Classical Greek styles and motifs. It was also a time of the lavish use of patterns and textures to embellish and enrich surfaces, both architectural and textile. Patterns were used alone, set off against a plain surface, or against other textures or patterns.

Classical Greek influence was important, but not the only inspiration for design. Spanish leather tooling motifs, called Strapwork were found on such different surfaces as furniture and the panes of trunk-hose, as well as the harnesses they were originally meant to ornament. Patterns from Persian carpets (so valuable that they were put on tabletops instead of the floor) found their way into weaving and decorative needlework. Some Chinese and East Indian influence was felt as well.

The English were especially fond of flowers and greenery (women often put nosegays into the tops of their bodices), and foliage is abundantly represented in the needlework of the time. Other motifs were mythical, fantastic beasts, as well as the fruits, birds, natural beasts, and insects of the English landscape surrounding them.

woven pattern

blackwork embroidery pattern

crewel embroidery motif

crewel embroidery motif

embroidery patterns

spanish strapwork pattern

Textile techniques must be divided into functional (spinning, weaving, knitting, and the beginnings of crochet), and purely decorative (embroidery and lacemaking). Whether your interests are in the functional techniques or the decorative, you might wish to add this to your research. We have seen some stunning re-creations of historical garments made from cloth spun and woven by hand, as well as hand-stitched and embellished. We have also seen courtier's suits lavished with blackwork or crewel embroidery as well as ruffs made from hand-made bobbin lace. These are definitely labors of love, but the results are worth it.

Embroidery techniques were practiced by any woman with a bit of spare time. Even peasant women found a little time to embroider to patch or darn a hole, as well as to cover stains. The finest work, however was done by those with the most free time to devote to it, that is, the upper classes. One of the most famous and skilled needlewomen of her time was Mary, Queen of Scots, who probably had more free time than most of her contemporaries, being a prisoner most of her adult life.

1. Blackwork (black thread worked over fine linen in intricate patterns, sometimes embellished with gold threads. One of the men's shirts show an example of this)
2. Crewel work (common even today)
3. Cuttework (threads in a piece of fabric are cut out and the resulting hole bound with white thread in stitches to form a design)
4. Pettit-point (similar to modern needlepoint, but worked on fine linen instead of coarse canvas)
5. Tapestry (a carry-over from the Middle Ages)
6. Stumpwork (embroidery over padding; the design becomes almost three-dimensional)

A few of these techniques are illustrated here and throughout the text.

blackwork embroidery pattern

petit-point pattern

stumpwork pattern

Surfaces covered were many and varied: bed hangings, chemises, shirts, coifs, purses, underskirt foreparts, sleeves, doublets, aprons, shoes, handkerchiefs, or whatever else would stand still long enough for it. The list is almost endless.

Lace was all made by hand at this time, so that only the very rich could afford to purchase it. Bobbin, fillet and needle lace were the types available. Crochet was not used for delicate things such as lace, and tatted lace was not yet known. Lacemaking itself was just getting its start as an art and industry.

Lace was often hand-made by upper class ladies for their use and that of their families, so is conceivable that a few of the sumptuous ruffs shown in portraits were made by the lady wearing it, or for a gentleman by his loving female relatives.

Lace was stronger, less delicate than in later periods, and was never found as a fabric. The widest hand-made lace was about three inches wide, and most edging lace was about one inch wide. A good lacer (a person who makes lace) can take up to two hours to make just one inch of bobbin lace in an intricate pattern, so it is obvious why only the wealthy could wear it. In order to make the wider lace ruffs seen later in the century, the lace was sewn together to make a wider strip.

ELIZABETHAN COLOR NAMES

Bristol-red --- a "pleasant" red
Cane color -- yellowish tint
Carnation -------------------------------- a color resembling raw flesh
Crane color --- a greyish white
Dead Spaniard --------------------------------------- a pale greyish tan
Gingerline -- reddish violet
Goose-turd -- yellowish green
Hair -- bright tan
Incarnate -- red
Isabella -- light buff
Lincoln green --- bright green
Lustie-gallant --- light red
Maiden hair --- bright tan
Milk-and-water --- bluish white
Murrey --- purplish red
Orange tawney --- orangish brown
Peach -- deep pinkish orange
Plunket --- light blue
Popinjay -- bluish green
Primrose --- pale yellow
Puke --- dirty brown
Rat's color --- dull grey
Sad --- any dark color
Sangyn --- blood red
Sheep's color -- natural
Strammel --- red
Straw --- light yellow
Tawney -- brown tinged with yellow
Watchet -- pale greenish blue
Whey -- pale whitish blue
Willow -- light green

SOME OTHER COLORS

Dove-grey	Tristami	Amaranth
Pansy	Flowering rye	Flax-blue
Scratch-face	Fading flower	Bottle-green
Verdigris	Gosling green	Judas-color
Dawn	Canary	Ox-blood
Water-color	Argentine	Dying monkey
Bean-blue	Merry widow	Brown bread
Ape's laugh	Resurrection	Mortal sin
Cristalline	Kiss-me-darling	Ham-color
Smoked ox	Chimney-sweep	Love-longings

TRICKS OF THE TRADE

There are a great many different techniques in sewing and pattern making. This chapter will explain a few of the most important ones, to help speed you on your way. If you are a professional seamstress and/or costumer, you will probably know most, if not all, of the information here, but you should probably read it anyway. Not even Edith Head knew it all.

This chapter, nay, this entire book, is really an informal primer on easy pattern drafting for the historical costumer. Our approach is a "seat of the pants" method, that will keep you focused more on the final garment, than pattern drafting as an end in itself. Many books and instructors talk about basic pattern blocks. They advocate drafting a set of these basic blocks, or slopers, before attempting to construct a full costume. If you are planning to spend your life as a professional costumer, pattern blocks will be an essential.

Elementary draping

We have found that unless you enjoy drafting, making this set of blocks first, can discourage an enterprising sewer from what we consider the real fun...making your ideas become a beautiful reality. As you go along, developing your skills, you may want to take a class or two in formal pattern drafting. But do not let the rules and formulas bog down your creativity at any time, only augment it.

The way you organize your sewing projects will show in the end results. We suggest the following schedule as a place to start. Embellish it, change it around, or make a new one to fit your own way of working as you go along.

1. Idea
2. Working sketches
3. Measurements
4. Pattern drafting and draping
5. Fitting muslin and other mock-ups
6. Figure yardage, trims, etc.
7. Purchase materials
8. Actual sewing, fitting, final touches
9. Applause

Advance planning helps to prevent mistakes, dispel nervousness, and will more than make up for time spent in this way.

Lace pattern

Ideas

Ideas can come from many sources. They can come from a book that you are reading, or a movie you just saw. You may see a painting or statue that you want to reproduce in cloth. You may have a secret yearning to look just like a famous character from song or story. You are costuming a play, or maybe Halloween is coming. The ideas can come from as many sources as there are people who want costumes.

When you are doing historical costuming, examine art sources to familiarize yourself with basic silhouettes, proportions, and typical details of the period. This will help make things go more smoothly.

Working drawing

178

Working Sketches

Your sketchbook will be your most important tool. When we talk about sketching, we don't mean professional quality finished drawings, only a type of visual shorthand. No matter how artistic you consider yourself to be, you can draw well enough to put your ideas on paper. Where will the trim go, how many buttons will there be down the front, is the front too fancy compared with the back? No one else ever needs to see these drawings. They are the first step in planning your project. Even if you are going to be copying a portrait exactly, you will still need to work out how you want the back to look. You can't turn that portrait around to see the back of the costume, after all.

Good working drawings will show the front, back and side views. It also can help to sketch, starting from the skin out. Drawing each layer as it will be put on, will help to visualize the total effect. Whenever there are unusual details, close-up drawings are crucial. A good rule of thumb is to sketch a tricky part over and over again, until you understand it. Paper and pencil are a lot cheaper than cloth.

Measurements

Taking measurements are done most smoothly, when you take your time. Don't be afraid to take the same measurements over and over if you feel unsure of yourself. Make up your own measurement sheet and follow it, attempting to formulate a method that works for you.

Body types vary

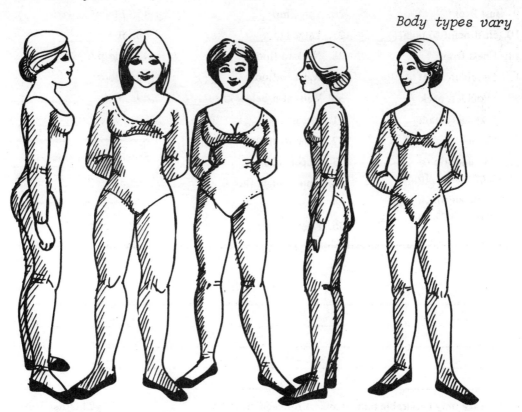

MEASUREMENT CHART

Dress size_____   Tights/stocking   Height_____   Name_____
                    size_____
Suit size_____   Weight_____   Phone_____
                    Hat size_____
Shirt_____   Hair_____   Project/Role_____
                    Shoe size_____
Pants waist_____   Eyes_____   _____
                    Handed_____
Pants inseam_____   Color preferences_____

1. Head around_____
2. Head over top_____
3. Neck_____
4. Neck height, front_____
5. Neck height, back_____
6. Bust_____
7. Chest_____
8. Bust front_____
9. Bust back_____
10. Bust point to point_____
11. Chest front_____
12. Shoulder, front_____
13. Shoulder, back_____
14. Shoulder, seam_____
15. Slope_____
16. Shoulder tip to
    center waist, front_____
17. Shoulder tip to
    center waits, back_____

18. Armscye front_____
19. Armhole, snug_____
20. Underarm seam_____
21. Waist_____
22. Neck to W. front_____
23. Neck to W. back_____
24. Hip @ bones_____
25. Hip to waist_____
26. Large hip_____
27. Large hip_____
28. Neck to floor_____
29. Waist to floor_____
30. Waist/just below knee_____
31. Inseam_____
32. Knee to ankle_____
33. Upper thigh_____
34. Upper thigh, flexed_____
35. Knee_____
36. Knee, flexed_____

37. Calf_____
38. Ankle_____
39. Overall rise_____
40. Rise front_____
41. Rise back_____
42. Arm length_____
43. Overarm_____
44. Arm to elbow_____
45. Elbow to wrist_____
46. Bicep_____
47. Bicep, flexed_____
48. Elbow_____
49. Wrist_____
50. Hand/fist_____

Special measurements:

_____

_____

_____

Notes: _____

_____

_____

_____

_____

Note: Take only applicable measurements for each project.   © 1983 Other Times Publications
Feel free to photocopy this sheet for your personal use.

180

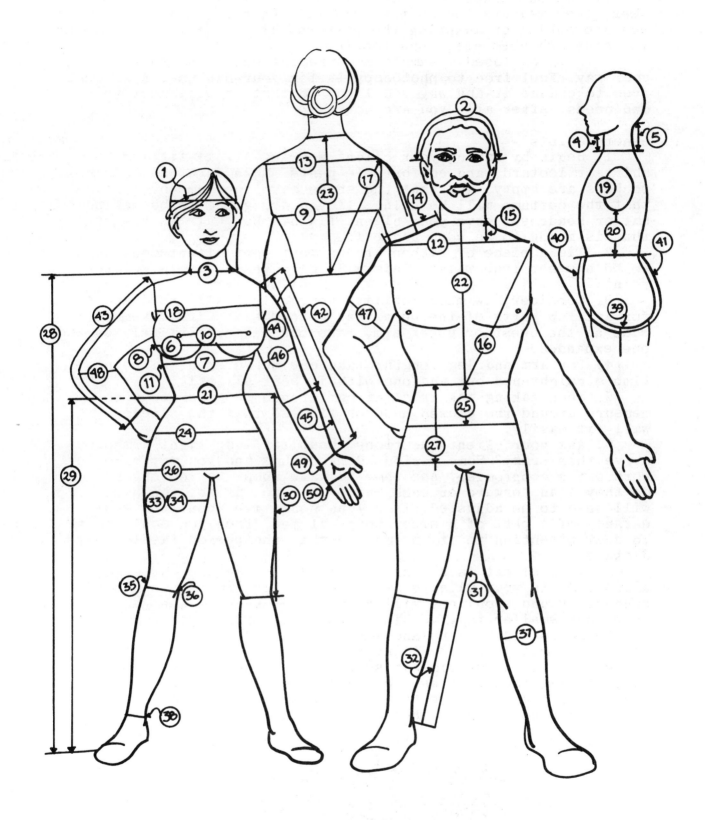

181

If someone takes your measurements for you, observe how and where they measure you so that you will be sure, later on, when you are making or adapting the pattern. It is far better to take too many measurements, than too few.

We have enclosed a sample measurement sheet to start you on your way. Feel free to photocopy it for your own use. Also feel free to change it any way you like, so that it will meet your own needs. After all, you are not us!

General Hints -

1. Begin by having your client wearing a well-fitting T-shirt or leotard, and comfortable pants. Make sure that his/her pockets are empty, and that the shoes have the same heel height that the costume will be using. If you are going to be making a hat or headress, have your client fix his/her hair in the style that is going to be worn under it.

2. Tie a piece of ribbon around what your client considers to be his/her true waist. This will give you a stable reference point.

3. Consider how much mobility your client will need and allow for it. For parts of the body that change size with movement, such as the chest or upper arm, take one measurement relaxed and one expanded.

4. For arm and leg length, take one measurement with the limb straightened out and one with it bent slightly.

5. When taking the wrist circumference remember to also measure around the closed hand or fist so that the sleeve will fit easily.

6. Ask your client questions about fit - do tight armholes drive them crazy? Some periods demand them and you may have to work out a compromise. Ask them to walk about as you observe - do they lean forward or back while moving - if so, the hems will need to be adjusted. Is he/she sensitive about the appearance of a part of his/her body; if yes, then you don't want to draw attention to it, no matter what the period fashion may dictate.

If your client is a singer or a dancer, severe corsetry is a problem. Is your clients back straight or are the shoulders rounded. Round shoulders will require the back of the garment to be cut smaller to give him/her a more upright posture.

These considerations and similar ones should be in your mind while measuring and talking with your client. Get your client to talk about him/her self. And let them know that you want to make them look as good as possible when they are wearing the costume you make for them. That sort of accomplishment can bring a costumer his/her greatest satisfaction.

Embroidery motif

Some tools will be necessary for this part of the job. If you sew at all, you probably have the basics, without having to go out and spend more money. You will need old grocery bags or newspapers to draw your patterns onto, a pair of paper-cutting scissors, pencils, clear or masking tape to make a large piece of paper larger, erasers (no one is perfect), a measuring tape, a ruler, a yardstick, and a right angle/45° triangle (inexpensive plastic, 8" on a side). You will also need a sizable flat surface, the kitchen table or your uncarpeted floor will do, and good lighting, so you won't strain your eyes.

As you get more involved, you may want to acquire the following tools and aids:

1. Magic markers or colored pencils; you should always start your pattern in one color, then use a new color for each successive correction.

2. Architectural sketch paper which can be found at most art supply stores. This is a type of inexpensive tracing paper, similar to commercial pattern paper, and comes on rolls of various widths. It has the added advantage of transparency, so that you can easily lay pattern pieces together to see how they fit, or to make a final tracing.

3. Newspaper end rolls are also quite cheap and widely available from any local newspaper office for very little money. You can unroll as much as you need and the cost is so low, you can afford to be generous with it.

4. You may prefer to use a roll of Butcher, or Kraft paper which is what grocery bags are made from. This is especially useful, if the patterns are going to be used a lot.

5. Other helpful drafting aids include French Curves, clear plastic rulers, 15"-18" long, marked off in 1/8" or 1/10" increments. For those metric-minded individuals, you might prefer one marked off in centimeters or milimeters. You may also want a T-square and a dressmaker's curve, but they are not essential.

Pattern-making hints -

1. Use commercial patterns as textbooks, and learn from them. Observe what different neck curves look like and how they fit. Notice the difference between armhole (armscye) and crotch (rise) curves front and back. This kind of observation will give you the insight necessary in applying a two-dimensional surface, the pattern, to a three-dimensional surface, the body.

Be aware that a commercial pattern can be wrong for you. Human beings design and make them, and they are prone to error. The human body that the garment industry uses as a standard, is just that, a standard. Most people vary from the standard in some respect.

2. Read a good, basic sewing text, especially the sections on how to correct patterns for figure faults. Observe, dispassionately, the person you will be sewing for. Note any irregularities in stance and proportion. Many people have one hip or shoulder slightly higher than the other, they are long or short waisted, big or small hipped, round-shouldered, sway-backed, or

pot-bellied. Unless you are striving for a particular character exaggeration, you will want to minimize these flaws.

3. The Fearsome Four: even experienced pattern drafters have difficulty in these areas. As you alter commercial patterns, make changes in these areas with great care. They are: the armhole (armscye) curve, the shoulder (slope) seam, the crotch (rise) curve, and the length from the armpit to the waist. This last one is a tough one to get right, yet it almost always has to be adjusted. This length is crucial in any closely fitting garment.

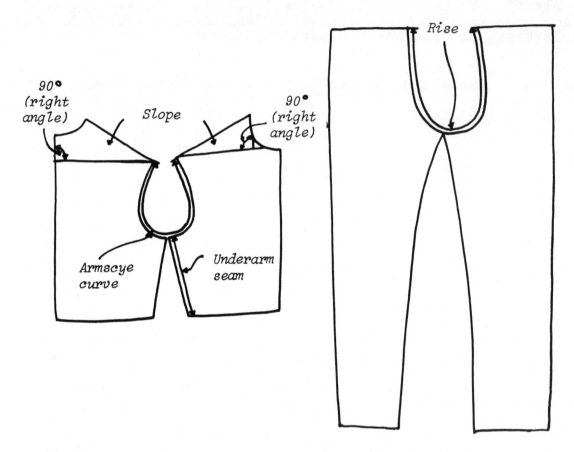

Draping -

This is a skill that most books assume you have. Books on the subject are rare, and classes rarer still. If your community college offers a class in draping, jump at the chance! The beautiful evening gowns of the 1920's and 30's were made almost entirely by draping the fabric to form the pattern.

In this part, we will show you the rudiments of the technique of draping. By no means, is what we show you, all the secrets of this useful art. The best part of experimenting with draping, is the information you will learn about pattern shape, and how it relates to the three-dimensional human body. As you go on, you will find that your eye will gain an education in visualizing how a sketch or pattern piece will look in the round.

Draping can be defined as laying either paper or cloth, usually muslin, directly on a dress form or human body, then pinning

1928 Draped gowns

and cutting until you have the shape and style you want, then
using this for a pattern base. The more you use this technique,
the more uses you will find for it. High collars, unusual neck-
lines, and sleeve treatments will be easier, when you experiment with draping. It can be done anytime during the pattern
drafting process to clarify and test ideas.

As with any technique, your attempts will be hit or miss;
some ideas won't work, no matter what. You will learn, and while
learning, you will be conserving the more expensive fabric. So
regard this as an adventure. It's fun!

The main drawback to this is that you will need access to a
dressmaker's form, or dress dummy. This is an advisable thing to

have around anyway, if you are planning to do any serious sewing, so shop around for the best value. A friend might be willing to loan you one for awhile, so if you are on a tight budget, this is the time to do some creative scrounging. Male forms are rare. We have an old pasteboard male torso dummy that we found in a store that wanted to dispose of it. So keep your eyes open.

We can't say it enough! Take your time! Think it through! Fit and drape, and allow yourself to walk away, if you get frustrated. If you learn anything from our experience, this is it. Working under pressure can cause you to make mistakes, so if you can't get rid of the pressure, be methodical.

Check how each seam relates to the other seams. Mark notes all over the draped piece. Mark any seams or details right on the drape, so when you unpin it, you will know what you have done. Since draping is a great way to work with bias-cut fabric, how the garment hangs is something to look at, as well.

Draping with paper to make a collar pattern is shown here below:

1. Lay the paper on the dummy and pin it in place.

2. Slash and refit the paper, so that it fits the form more closely. Keep doing this, until it seems to be right.

3. Sketch on the paper the proposed collar. If any of the slashes intrude into the area of the collar, tape over them, so that when the paper is removed, the slashes will stay spread. Mark the center front and back, seam areas, allowances, and grainline.

4. Remove the drape and squash flat. Smooth out any rough areas in the curves, and trim away the excess paper.

5. Redraw the pattern on a clean piece of paper, and make a mock-up to check for fit. If necessary, repeat any of the preceding steps until you are satisfied.

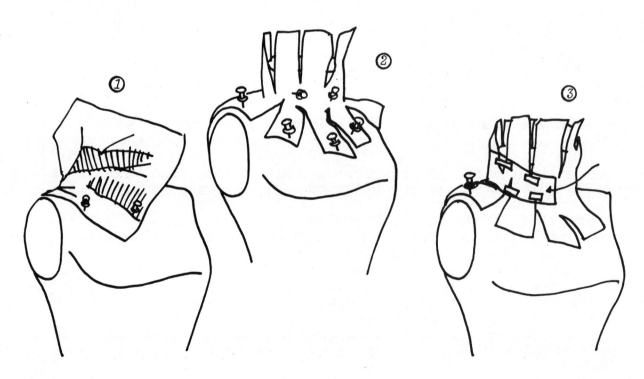

186

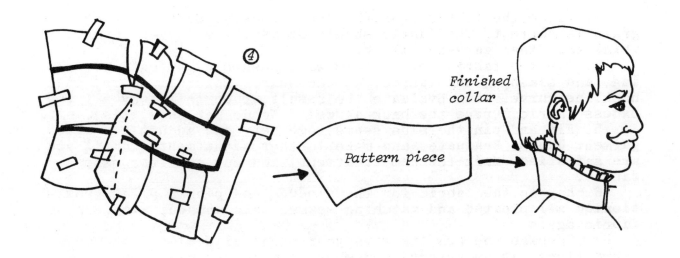

Finished collar

Pattern piece

The next example we show is NOT A HISTORICAL GARMENT. We designed it to help illustrate a simple garment that would be difficult to visualize as a flat pattern without draping as an intermediate step.

1. Do a detailed design. Remember to draw both front and back of the design.

2. Locate a logical starting point. This will be a stable neckline, as shown here, or another feature upon which the rest of the garment depends for a base. We have draped the collar in place, pinning it securely.

3. Place the fabric over the dummy, making sure that the grain is correct. The fabric should be a little larger than you think the final garment will be.

4. Pin the fabric to the form with push pins, pleating, folding, and slashing the fabric, as necessary. Mark all seams, grain, neckline curve, etc. Evaluate the result, then trim away all the excess fabric. Drape the back as well (We do not show this).

5. Fit and pin the side seams together, and adjust how the garment hangs. Evaluate, and make further adjustments, until you are satisfied. Mark the hem treatment, and cut away the excess fabric.

6. Lay on the fabric for the sleeve, and pin in place, positioning all pleats, and matching seams. Mark and cut away excess fabric again.

7. Compare the results with your original design. Make any corrections, as necessary. Remember to make any notes on the drape now, before removing it. Take the drape off of the form, carefully removing all the pins. This is your pattern. Make a mock-up next; real bodies differ from stiff manikins, even if they have the same measurements.

The last draping technique we will show, is also the easiest. We've used it for shoes and boots, hosen, leather jerkins, and Victorian mitts. Always use a protective base. Remember how band-aids feel when they are ripped off. Bases can be an old sock, a glove, nylons, or a T-shirt, whatever will suit your purpose.

1. Make a design (in this case, a boot)
2. Put on your base (an old sock)
3. Wrap masking tape or duct tape around and around, covering the base completely, but not too tightly.
4. Cut it off carefully, along where you will want the seam lines to be. This is now your pattern. Add seam allowances after squashing it flat and redrawing it. Make a mock-up and fit it. If you are working with leather which will be laced together, omit the seam allowances.
5. Now, wasn't that easy?

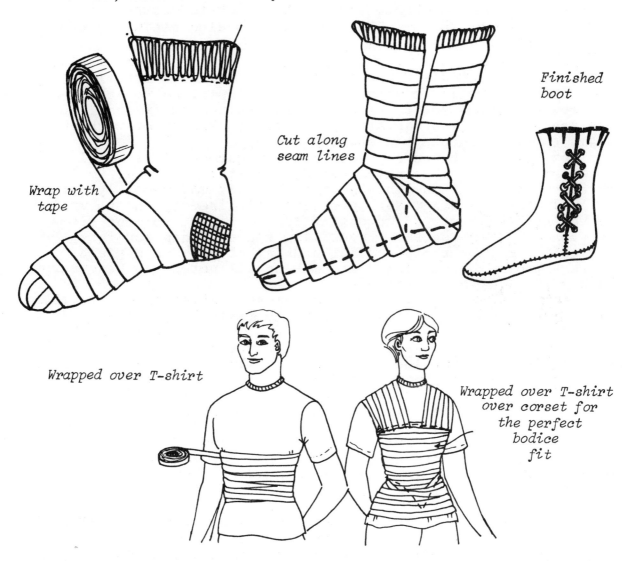

Wrap with tape

Cut along seam lines

Finished boot

Wrapped over T-shirt

Wrapped over T-shirt over corset for the perfect bodice fit

Our last word on this is, Experiment! There is no limit to what you can achieve with a few techniques and a creative, courageous approach. You can do it!

The word "muslin" refers to a rough, sample garment made to test the fit of a pattern. They are most often made of an inexpensive cotton cloth, called muslin, hence the name.

Never underestimate this step. It can save you a lot of grief since you can check your pattern before you cut into your $20 per yard wool or velvet. Remember that this step is meant to save you money, so pick a lightweight, inexpensive cloth. Muslin on sale can cost you as little as 50¢ a yard. Old sheets are also useful, if you have any you are willing to sacrifice. Some seamstresses use tissue paper and tape, but this is fragile, and doesn't have the give and drape of cloth.

Another material that is sometimes used for muslins is non-woven interfacing. This is best for simulating how leather will work, since you can choose the weight which is closest to the leather you want to use. This material is also useful to construct muslins for confining garments, such as corsets and tight-fitting bodices. It is too expensive for other pattern making purposes, and doesn't drape at all well, being too stiff.

Making a muslin is easy. Just use the pattern to cut it out and sew the seams together without fastenings or facings. Leave one seam open so you can struggle into it. Put it on with the seams exposed and pin the opening closed.

Now, step back and evaluate how the garment fits. Is it too tight or too loose. Wrinkles can denote stress points, so look for those too. The muslin should fit evenly and smoothly, without bulges or binding. Mark your changes directly on the muslin, so you won't forget. If something is too tight, you can slash it evenly, and measure the resulting spaces. When you take the garment off, pick the seams out and lay it down on a piece of pattern paper. Trace around it, making all notes, as necessary. This will be your new pattern.

Very complex, or form-fitting garments often take more than one muslin to assure a good fit in the final form. If you are going to set in a sleeve, only do one sleeve, so you can check both the armhole and shoulder fit, and see how the sleeve works.

For more information on fitting problems, and how to correct for them, consult a good, basic sewing text. Observation is your key to a good fit, so look at it closely. Then step back and keep in mind that the final fabric will have a different "hand" (how it hangs, how heavy it is), and remember to allow for it.

If the muslin you are making is for yourself, it must be fitted onto your body be another person, and you should choose someone with a skill level close to your own, or better, in order to avoid problems. Also, do it in front of a mirror, so that you can direct them.

There are other types of mock-ups besides muslins. Cutting miniature patterns out of paper to test pleating patterns and adjustments, is a good preliminary step to making a full sized pattern. Some people make doll clothes to test their ideas. It allows them to see how things will look together, such as color schemes, without going into too much detail. If you are planning

Play with the muslin!

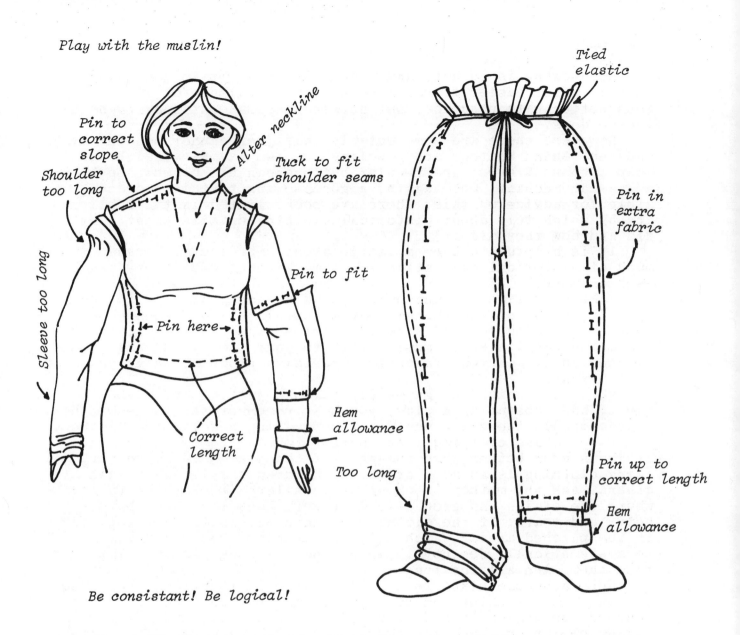

Pin to correct slope

Shoulder too long

Alter neckline

Tuck to fit shoulder seams

Sleeve too long

Pin to fit

Pin here

Correct length

Hem allowance

Too long

Tied elastic

Pin in extra fabric

Pin up to correct length

Hem allowance

Be consistant! Be logical!

to make doll clothes, that's fine. But since dolls are not proportioned like real people, you may find that this method lacks something in reality.

Anyway, these are just a few ideas to help you work out your own ideas. Be inventive and come up with some of your own. What you want to do is explore your ideas, before you commit your time and effort, as well as money, to them.

The rest of this book is about sewing the specific garments. So our last piece of advice offered here is to become a list maker. Decide what kind of order will work best for you so you can finish your project with your temper and your pocketbook still intact. Then write it down. As you finish that step, cross it off. That will help you to budget your time, and it feels so good to cross off the next item on your list as you finish it.You can chart your progress, and eventually, you will cross off the last item. Hurrah!

Final Details

Handsewing is an art, and like most arts, it is something that is a lot easier if you have a natural talent for it. It gets better with practice, but nothing can make it fun. We hates it, we does.

However, there are some details that just cannot be done by machine. Shank buttons and jeweling are two examples, although snaps, hooks & eyes, and regular buttons can all be sewn on by a zig-zag machine. Once again, a good sewing text is indespensible for advice on this. There are books listed in the bibliography which tell about historical clothing details (what they did and how they did it).

It is helpful to know a little about embroidery, because so much of historical decoration was some kind of embroidery, such as blackwork.

Take your time on handsewing, beading and jeweling, if you can. It is one of the things that makes all the difference between a slapdash job and a really professional quality piece of work. You can listen to music, talk to your family and friends, or keep an eye on your favorite television program, while you stitch away.

When you finish the garment, it looks just great, maybe too great. When costuming a play, you must remember that some of the characters in the story would not be wearing new-looking clothes.

Lower class clothing looks better, when it doesn't look new. It looks even better when the ages of the pieces seem to vary. Aging clothing is an art, at which children excell, above all others. Ask any mother. Look at used children's clothing to see where the stains and ground-in dirt are. Look for worn spots, holes and tears. If the clothes are patched, is there fresh wear in the patched areas? Watch children at play. See what they do to systematically destroy their clothes. You can learn a lot from them. And all for free.

Here are some hints to achieve that well-worn look. Repeated washings in hot water and strong soap are a good place to start. You did pre-shrink your fabric before you cut it, didn't you? Adding bleach or washing soda will help to speed the aging process, but be careful not to add too much. It will age the fibers too rapidly and the garment will fall apart with the first wearing. The sun is your ally, if you have enough time to let the garment sit out in the sun (and the rain) for the effect.

One of our friends swears by, first putting the garment on, walking into the ocean with it, then letting it dry on her body. Effective, but itchy. Some people have run over a garment or dragged it behind their car to age it.

To simulate stains, coffee, red wine, strong tea, and diluted acrylic paint will work very well. Sandpaper is good for abrading areas that would show wear, such as knees, elbows, seat and seams. Fading patches on faded cloth also works. Man-made fabrics don't age as gracefully as natural fibers, so be aware, and don't get too agressive. You don't want to have to start all over again, do you?

The subject never mentioned enough in any book on costuming is the phase after all the sewing and detailing is done. Enjoy the fruits of your labor. Wear it often and become familiar with it. Your costume will, in time, develop a personality, and probably a nickname of its own. It will never be finished. Every time you wear it, you may add accessories or other details.

This phase of costuming will educate you as much as any other while you discover what works and what doesn't. Continue to evaluate your efforts. That way, each time you create something, it will be easier and more fun. Nobody really does this only for the money.

We hope that these ideas will speed you on your way to success, and that you will never stop learning.

"We love our new costumes, Mommy!"

GENERAL PATTERN SECTION & YARDAGES

There are no modern commercial patterns for doublets, slashed sleeves, or flat-fronted bodices. This may tend to create a real problem for those of you who need some kind of a pattern to build on, or you want a short-cut.

This section is intended to picture and describe several representative pattern types for your delight and edification. The pull-out section from the first edition, which listed specific pattern numbers was a good idea, but turned out to be too cumbersome and impractical in practice. Pattern numbers change too quickly, but certain basic pattern types remain fairly constant.

References are made to these pattern types within the text of the how-to sections and they are illustrated here to help make your life less complicated. We suggest that you try to find a pattern that looks like one of the basic types you may need, in one of the current editions of the commercial pattern books found at every fabric store.

Then you can make any of the necessary alterations to the pattern according to the instructions given in the text of each section.

In the last part of this chapter, we will give yardages for all of the garments contained in this book. These yardages are based on an average-sized person; that is to say, size 12-14 and 5'6" for a woman, and size 38-40 and 6' for a man. These yardages are meant only as general guidelines to aid you in your planning. Your actual yardages may differ, due to size and style considerations for what you will be making.

Some garments and accessories described in the text are easy to make without any commercial pattern. We have listed them below. Just consult the instructions in the appropriate section.

Aprons	Farthingales
Bumrolls	Hats and Headresses
Capes, long/short	Ruffs
Corsets	Skirts

Some items are purchased, then altered or added to in order to make them more closely resemble period pieces:

Eyeglasses	Jewelry
Fans	Shoes
Gloves	Stockings

GENERAL PATTERN SHAPES

Men's Drawstring Pants

Men's Standard Shirt

Men's French-cut Shirt

Men's Simple Over-vest

Men's Suitcoat

Women's Peasant Blouse

Clown's Suit

Women's Standard Blouse

Men's Vest

Women's Vest

Women's Basic Bodices

YARDAGES

All yardages assume 45" wide fabric unless otherwise specified.

Men's Clothing

Shirts, all variations, fabric	4
interfacing	½
Breeches, fabric	2½
interfacing	¼
Venetians, fabric	2–3
interfacing	¼
Trews, cross-gartered, fabric	2½
Canions, fabric and lining	1½ ea
Trunk-hose or Slops, panes, lining, contrast, lining	1½ ea
interfacing	3
net for stuffing	3–5
Pansied Slops, panes, lining, contrast	1½ ea
interfacing	3
net for stuffing	2–3
Jerkin, fabric and optional lining	1–2 ea
Doublet, plain and noble's, fabric and lining (not including sleeves)	2½–3 ea
interfacing	½–3
Doublet, middle class, fabric and lining	3–3½ ea
interfacing	½–1
Doublet, peascod-bellied, fabric and lining	3–3½ ea
interfacing	3–4
net for stuffing	2–3
Short capes, ½ circle, fabric and lining	2½ ea
¾ circle, fabric and lining	3½ ea
Surcote or Cape-coat, fabric and lining	6–7 ea
Schaube, sleeve fabric and lining	2 ea
body & yoke fabric and lining	3 ea
collar and revers	1½
Scholar's Gown, fabric etc. as for schaube plus	2–3

Women's Clothing

Shift and Partlet, hip length	.4–4½
Shift, ankle length	5–6
Over-partlet/Italian Partlet	½–1
Petticoat	3½–4
Bumroll	½
Corset, fabric and lining	½–1
interfacing	1–2
Farthingale, fabric	2½–3
1" binding or ribbon, hoopwire	12–15 ea
Skirts, plain and gored (36" wide fabric)	.4½–5
(45" wide fabric)	4–4½
Upper class Underskirt (36" wide fabric)	4–5
(45" wide fabric)	3–4
Bodice, fabric and lining (not including sleeves)	.1–1½ ea
interfacing	2–3

Spanish Surcote, fabric and lining	5–7 ea
interfacing	2–3

Unisex Clothing Parts and Accessories

Sleeves, fabric and lining	.1½–3 ea
interfacing (as required)	2–4
Long Cape or Cloak, fabric and lining	5–8
Hats and headresses, coif or biggins	¼–½
Head drapes	½–1
Attifet	½
Muffin cap	1
Caul	½–1
Flat cap	1½
Biretta	1–1½
Beguin (Windsock)	1½
French Hoods	½
Veils	1–1½
Tall Hat	1
Pillbox type	½
Ruffs, simple separate box-pleated type (lace)	2–3
accordion-pleated, including variations	4–6
circle type	3
Cloth Hosen	2–3
Garters, ribbon or length of cloth strip	.1½–2
Pouches, drawstring or belt type	¼
Children's clothes	depends on ages and sizes

SOURCES

For those of you who lack access to many necessary sewing supplies, we offer several useful West Coast sources for many of them. We have listed West Coast sources because we live and work in California, and have managed to find everything we need locally. If you put out a little extra effort, you should be able to find sources in your own area. If you find some particularly good sources, please let us know, so we can add them next time. Good luck to you.

Ethnic & historical patterns -
   Folkwear Patterns
   P.O. Box 3859, Dept EC
   San Rafael, CA 94912

   Retail mail order, wholesale inquiries/$1.00 for catalog; fascinating patterns from history, nicely wearable, reasonably priced

Lace, corset stays -
   Lacis
   2990 Adeline St.
   Berkeley, CA 94703
   (415)843-7178

   Retail, wholesale, walk-in & mail order/catalog available; a treasure trove of the unique in lace both antique & modern, hand-made & machine made, corset stays, unusual sewing supplies, books & patterns

Dyes & yarns -
   Straw into Gold
   3006 San Pablo Ave.
   Berkeley, CA 94702
   (415)548-5241

   Retail, prefers walk-in to mail orders/$1.00 for catalog; fabric dyes, both immersible & paint-on, yarns, spinning & weaving supplies, some trims, books, worth a visit, very friendly & helpful

Thread, notions -
   Acme Thread
   826 S. Los Angeles St.
   Los Angeles, CA 90014
   (213)680-0860

   Retail, wholesale, $25 minimum, C.O.D. or cash, walk-in & mail order/no catalog; large (2000 & 6000 yd) spools of thread, safety pins, rayon hem binding, elastic in 100 yd rolls

Boning, hook tape -
   Fine Brand, Inc.
   300 East 4th St.
   Los Angeles, CA 90013
   (213)629-1449

   Wholesale only, no minimum, walk-in & mail order/no catalog; hook tape in white, black & ecru, boning sold in dozens in each size ($\frac{1}{4}$" & $\frac{1}{2}$" wide, 3"-18" long in $\frac{1}{2}$" increments)

Trims, buttons -
   Handcraft from Europe
   P.O. Box 372
   Sausalito, CA 94965
   (415)332-1633

   Retail mail order, no minimum, walk-in (call first)/no catalog; gold & silver non-tarnish trims, specialty trims, send sample to match, needlework supplies, buttons

Beads & findings -
   Berger's Specialty Company
   413 East 8th St.
   Los Angeles, CA 90014
   (213)627-8783

   Retail, wholesale, walk-in & mail order/no catalog; beads, jewels (glue-on & sew-on), findings, including aglets; all sold by the gross, 100s, or by the yard, as applicable

Millinery supplies -
   Leon Berlin
   707 Broadway
   Los Angeles, CA 90014
   (213)622-7064

   Prefer wholesale, walk-in & mail order/no catalog; hat wire, buckram, hat pins (3" & 8"), by the gross or by the yard

Feathers -
   Am Can Feathers
   8344 Beverly Blvd.
   Hollywood, CA 90048
   (213)653-1508

   Retail, wholesale, walk-in & mail order/no catalog; maribou, pheasant (mostly by 100s), ostrich (best by the pound), feather dying to order, other special services available on request

Ribbons, trims -
   Offray Ribbon
   805 East Pico
   Los Angeles, CA 90014
   (213)747-9668

   Wholesale only, walk-in & mail order, minimum 10 yds each color, C.O.D. or cash/catalog on request; supplier to most fabric stores

BIBLIOGRAPHY

Most of these books will be available in your public library and some of them are still in print, so may be purchased, if you wish to add them to your collection. An * by the title means that it is especially useful.

Batterberry, Michael & Ariane, *Fashion: The Mirror of History.* Chanticleer Press/ Crown Publishers, Hong Kong, 1977.

*Boucher, Francois, *20,000 Years of Fashion.* Harr Abrams, New York, 1966.

Bradfield, Nancy, *Historical Costumes of England—11th to 20th Century.* George Harrap & Co., Ltd., London, 1963.

*Braune & Schneider, *Historic Costume in Pictures.* Dover Publications, New York, 1975.

Brooke, Iris, *English Costume in the Age of Elizabeth.* Adam & Charles Black, London, 1973.

*Bruhn & Tilke, *A Pictorial History of Costume.* Frederick A Praeger, New York, 1955.

Calthrop, Dion, *English Costume 1066–1820.* Adam & Charles Black, London, 1963.

Castiglione, Baldesar, *The Book of the Courtier.* Anchor Books, New York, 1959.

Chapman, Suzanne E., *Historic Floral and Animal Designs for Embroidery and Craftsmen.* Dover Publications, New York, 1977.

Contini, Mila, *Fashion from Ancient Egypt to the Present Day.* Odyssey Press, New York, 1965.

Cunnington, Phyllis, *Costume in Pictures.* E. P. Dutton & Co., New York, 1964.

*Cunnington, C. Willit & Phyllis, *Handbook of English Costume in the Sixteenth Century.* Faber & Faber Ltd., London, 1970.

Davenport, Elsie, *Your Handspinning.* Craft & Hobby Book Service, Pacific Grove, CA, 1964.

*Davenport, Milia, *The Book of Costume* (One volume edition). Crown Publishers, New York, 1948.

Fraser, Antonia, *Mary, Queen of Scots.* Delacorte Press, New York, 1969

Gorsline, Douglas, *What People Wore.* Bonarya Books, New York, 1952.

*Handford, Jack, *Professional Patternmaking for Designers of Women's Wear.* Burgess Publishing Co., New York, 1974.

*Hill & Bucknell, *The Evolution of Fashion 1066–1930.* Drama Book Specialists, New York, 1967.

Holmes, Martin, *Elizabethan London.* Praeger Publishers, New York, 1971.

Ingham & Covey, *The Costumer's Handbook.* Prentice-Hall, Inc., New York, 1980.

Jenkins, Elizabeth, *Elizabeth the Queen.* Coward McCann, New York, 1958.

Knill, Ellen, *Queen Elizabeth I Paper Dolls.* Bellerpheron Books, San Francisco CA, 1973.

Kunz, George Frederick, *Rings for the Finger.* Dover Publications, New York, 1973.

Kybalova, Ludmila, *The Pictorial Encyclopedia of Fashion.* Crown Publishers, New York, 1968.

*Laver, James; Editor, *Costumes of the Western World: Fashions of the Renaissance.* Harper & Bros., New York, 1951.

Lister, Margo, *Costumes of Everyday Life.* Barrie & Jenkins, London, 1972.

Luke, Mary, *A Crown for Elizabeth.* Coward McCann & Geoghegan, New York, 1970.

*Norris, Henry, *Costume and Fashion: Volume 3, Book 2.* J. M. Dent & Sons, Ltd., London, 1938.

Oaks & Hill, *Rural Costume: Origin and Development.* B. T. Batsford, Ltd., Great Britain, 1970.

Orlandi, Enzo, *The Life & Times of Elizabeth I.* Curtis Publishers, Philadelphia PA, 1966.

Petersen & Svennas, *Handbook of Stitches.* Van Nostrand Reinhold Co., New York, 1970.

Selbie, Robert, *The Anatomy of Costume.* Crescent Books, U.S., 1977.

Smith, Lacey Baldwin, *The Horizon Book of the Elizabethan World.* American Heritage Publishing Co., New York, 1967.

*Stone, George C., *Glossary of Arms and Armor.* Jack Brussel Publisher, New York, 1934 & 1961.

Strong & Oman, *Elizabeth R.* Stein & Day Publishers, New York, 1972.

Strong & Oman, *Mary Queen of Scots.* Stein & Day Publishers, New York, 1972.

Vecelio, Cesare, *Vecellio's Renaissance Costume Book.* Dover Publications, Canada, 1977.

Vinciolo, Federico, *Renaissance Patterns for Lace, Embroidery, and Needlepoint.* Dover Publications, New York, 1971.

Vogue Magazine Editors, *The Vogue Sewing Book.* Butterick Publishing, 1975 & 1982.

Wilcox, R. Turner, *The Mode of Costume.* Charles Scribner & Sons, New York, 1958.

Wilcox, R. Turner, *The Mode in Hats & Headress.* Charles Scriber & Sons, New York, 1959.

Williams, Neville, *All the Queen's Men.* Cardinal, Great Britain, 1974.

Wilson, Eunice, *A History of Shoe Fashions.* Pitman Publishing, London; Theater Arts Books, New York, 1974.

Worrell, Estelle, *Early American Costume.* Stackpole Books, Harrisburg PA, 1975.

Yarwood, Doreen, *English Costume: From 200 B.C. to 1960.* B. T. Batsford, Ltd., London, 1961.

Znamierowski, Nell, *Step by Step Weaving.* Golden Press, New York, 1967.

blackwork embroidery pattern

AFTERWORD

Now that you have dressed yourself in the garments of the time of Elizabeth I, we leave you with a description of the common form of greeting known as a reverance or bow. It is taken from a book by Thoinot Arbeau, published in 1588.

"To perform the reverance, you will keep the left foot firmly on the ground, and bending the right knee, carry the point of the toe a little to the rear of the left foot, at the same time doffing your bonnet or hat and saluting your damsel and the company, as you see in this picture. When the reverance has been performed, straighten the body, and replace your bonnet: then, advancing your right foot, bring and keep the two feet together. The reverance done, assume a goodly modest attitude."